A BIT OF FRENCH STICK

SALLY PATTINSON

Edited by Elizabeth Hojlund
Contact: info@elizabethhojlund.com

Acknowledgements

Special thanks

I would like to say a special thank you to all those young French people back in the 90's who supported the Malice shop and the Rockstocks, helped us at the markets and the Lille Braderies, taught me to speak French, and searched their memoir boxes to provide photos and memorabilia for this book.

Many thanks to Liliane and Serge for feeding us every Wednesday.

Thanks to Tom for creating the cover.

Thanks to Elizabeth for her help in editing

Contents

IN MEMORY OF

PIERROT, EDDIE, MARC EM, BABAS AND RAB

By Sally Pattinson

Chapter 1 - The Arrival

We arrived in Calais at 6.30 a.m. on March 18th, 1990, full of excitement at the huge step we had taken in moving across the channel to a new life full of hope or despair. Husband was working on the Channel Tunnel at Shakespeare Cliff near Dover and had tired of the daily journey from Hastings, so in his infinite wisdom had suggested we move to France for a better life. Having sold the house, husband, my 10 year old son, Annie the staff, three Persian cats and myself upped and left England and sadly my daughter too as she was in the middle of her A-levels at college and was going to stay the duration with my parents.

We had chosen to have a house built in a pretty location just outside Boulogne in a small hamlet called Wierre Effroy, in the little commune known as Le Trou d'Enfer which translates to The Hole of Hell. So while the house was under construction we rented a farmhouse from Monsieur Fevrier who was building our house. Samer is a small market town sixteen and a half kilometres south of Boulogne. We had to settle into our accommodation quickly as husband was only having six days with us before he went back to work. I needed a car as I had sold my fabulous black Ford Capri before we left so the priority was to buy me a car. It was a Ford Granada and it was the first time I had driven a left-hand drive car on the right side of the road at the same time and I was terrified. Anyway all was well and apart from driving through a red traffic light I soon became confident in what I was doing.

I put Tom into the local primary school within a week of us arriving in France. He didn't like it but he had to go to school, and whether he understood the lessons or not, he had to start sooner rather than later. Husband went back to work and there we were, Tom and I alone in a foreign country unable to speak a word of French. Horror: as soon as we had been left alone I could smell gas and I didn't know what to do. The only people I knew were the head mistress of Tom's school and Monsieur Chouchoi, who had sold us the Granada, and neither spoke a word of English, but we had exchanged addresses and phone numbers with Monsieur Chouchoi so he was our only option of rescue before the imminent gas explosion. I got the dictionary and looked up each word I needed to say: 'Aidez moi j'ai un poireau dans ma gaz butel'. I had no idea if that was correct or not but I practised saying it a few times and then rang Monsieur Chouchoi...I said my piece and understood not one word of his reply but I got a feeling he was coming to our rescue. It was pouring with rain with gale force winds and he turned up at the front door like a drowned rat only to be greeted by Annie the little staff who proceeded to jump all over the poor man and terrorize him. Having parted the dog from our saviour I led him into the house. He soon realized the problem; the cooker was attached to a gas bottle which had a double connection but as there was only one gas bottle attached the gas was leaking out of the spare connector. He screwed the vacant connection closed and all was well. I thanked him profusely and he left rather quickly back into the storm that was raging outside.

The house was freezing, with one open fireplace in the living area and wall to wall concrete upstairs, while downstairs it was tiled. There was plenty of land with the farmhouse, including the resident donkey called Alibaba, who lived a solitary life in one of the fields. One day a few weeks later when the weather was warming up I noticed that Alibaba had escaped his field and had broken into a field of cows. To my horror he was chasing and then mounting them. What could I do? Nothing! I was not going to enter the field with an over sexed donkey running amok in a herd of cows who were stampeding to get out of his way. So back to the dictionary, 'L'ane fait l'amour avec les vaches' on the phone to Monsieur Fevrier the landlord. What I was actually telling him was that 'the donkey was making love to the cows'. He understood and he soon arrived, wearing a suit and tie, and attempted to usher Alibaba back to his own field. Easier said than done! Monsieur Fevrier spent all afternoon chasing the donkey round and round the field of cows and could not catch him; it was a sight to behold. Poor Monsieur Fevrier, who was normally so immaculately dressed and clean, was covered in mud and other farm animal delights, as I could smell. He was totally bedraggled and sweating profusely, and his thick, normally well-groomed hair was all over the place. Finally he managed to get a rope round the donkey's neck and lead him back to his field.

Monsieur Fevrier chasing Ali BaBa the donkey

Me having a moment with Ali Baba

We gradually settled into the French way of life and although learning nothing at school Tom and I would sit down every evening and with the help of French for Beginners books we slowly learnt vocabulary and verbs. Husband would come home once every other weekend.

In June I received a letter from my father telling me that they could no longer have Lorraine living with them as she was a teenager and moody, so that was the end of her A-levels and over to France she came. She attended a lycée in Boulogne - the equivalent of a college in England. Her ambition was to be a teacher; she had French GCSE and spoke and wrote French very well, but sadly it was impossible for her to do a teaching course so she ended up doing a management course which did not appeal to her.

One hot summer's day in Samer we were relaxing in the tranquillity of the French countryside having cheese and baguettes, washed down with a fine glass of wine, in the garden enjoying the life, when a commotion came from one of the barns. Tom was hollering and all of a sudden pandemonium ensued, and he came tearing out of the barn towards us with the head of a dead rabbit on a spade followed closely by Annie with the body of the poor thing in her mouth. Lorraine, forever squeamish, screamed at the sight and tried to put her whole body onto the small garden chair in which she was sitting. Tom purposely ran revolutions round the table and the dog chased him until Tom tripped and went crashing into the table and the head of the rabbit fell off the spade. In the meantime Annie, realising the chase had come to an end, ate her half of the rabbit. Tom got up and pushed the head round the floor trying to hoick it back onto the spade until I ordered him to go and fling the damn thing into the field. After which we carried on with our lunch.

The house during construction

The new house was coming along quickly and I was excited to get in it ... and in August it was built and ready for us to move into. Husband moved us in over a weekend and then returned to work, leaving us in chaos with a huge number of boxes to unpack and furniture to arrange. The house was just a shell, with no kitchen apart from a sink. We did buy a new cooker and eventually he fitted a kitchen. The garden was 1/3 of an acre but it was a field front and back; there wasn't even a driveway. The end of the garden had no fence and adjoined the farmer's field. A makeshift driveway made of crushed gravel, that I think should have been turned into concrete, was just chucked down, and the idea was that the car would push it down to make it stick together.

Slowly, slowly things got done.

Tom was at school in Boulogne. Back home I used to dread his parents' evenings whereas I would be so proud of Lorraine's. His teachers would always moan about him and if he was sent out of the class, he would either walk out backwards slowly blinking, pretending to be in a trance, or sideways pretending to be Quasimodo and calling for Esmeralda. He had started to learn the drums when he was eight years old. I had bought him an old drum kit from a war-time friend of my father's. They had been in a band together. My father played the saxophone and clarinet and his friend Inky the drums. Tom took to drumming instantly and we had engaged a teacher for him who came once a week and now, once again, we were lucky to find another drum teacher for him in Boulogne. He would practise every day and I made it his priority so when he had homework I sent him to drum whilst I did the homework.

By the time Tom was thirteen his drumming was amazing and he wanted to be in a band, so we advertised for musicians in the local free newspaper. He was inundated with applicants, all playing their guitars and singing down the phone. So he invited the best sounding ones to come and audition. They turned up with their instruments and speakers and cables and all went up into Tom's bedroom. He chose Arno, age 19, as lead guitar, Guti, age 20 as bass guitar and Rab, age 27, a singer from Scotland. I said they could practise in his bedroom. So the rock band 'Malice in Wonderland' was forged.

By 1993 I was more confident with speaking French, although I still rarely went anywhere without a dictionary. I needed to get a job and there were already 3 million French people unemployed, so with the help of our neighbour Edith we compiled an advert which I put in the local free paper, 'Lady with car available for domestic duties', and my phone number. I was a bit concerned that I would struggle to converse successfully on the phone but that would remain to be seen. When the phone rang I said 'Bonjour'... There was a man on the other end, and I couldn't understand much of what he was saying but the bit I did understand was that he had a lingerie shop in Boulogne. I was puzzled! Did he want it cleaning I wondered? The conversation got nowhere so I gave up and put the phone down. The second caller was also a man, and he asked what colour my bra was! Unthinking, I looked and suddenly realised he was some kind of weirdo and hung up. My enthusiasm to find a job was starting to dwindle. However, there was a third caller, again a man, who asked me if I wore tampons or towels! I didn't even answer that one. I was shocked. All I wanted was a cleaning job and only perverts had responded. The fourth and final call was again a man, and as I answered the phone I could hear him breathing and didn't understand what he was saying. The breathing got louder and to my horror I realised he was masturbating down the phone, so I told him to 'piss off' to which he replied 'oh yes oh yes oh yes" breathing faster and faster and louder and louder. 'Say it again' he gasped.

I didn't say it again, I slammed the phone down.

Chapter 2 - Lessons to be Learnt

When the house was being constructed it had been fitted with a 'fosse septique', a septic tank in the garden. We had been told not to flush our sanitary products down the toilet, but in England we had the choice of disposable pads so Lorraine and I just carried on disposing down the toilet and thinking nothing of it. One hot day in the middle of summer I noticed the toilets weren't flushing away properly and there were gurgling noises coming from somewhere. A few flushes later I realised there was a problem with the sanitary system.

In France every town and village has a mayor, and in the country it is the mayor's privilege to empty the fosse septique for which you pay 350 francs. The mayor sells the contents of your fosse septique to the local farmers for 350 francs who then spray it all over their crops creating a stench from hell but huge tasty vegetables.

I drove to the village to the mayor's house and asked if they would come and empty the fosse septique. I was told that as the house was only 2 years old it shouldn't need emptying as normally it would be every 5 years, but I insisted that they should come and check anyway.

Later on two farm workers with cigarettes in their mouths turned up on a tractor towing a large tank with a large hose pipe wrapped round it. They drove the tractor right up to the side of the house where Lorraine and I were waiting to greet them. They asked where the fosse septique was, but I hadn't a clue. They proceeded to walk around the back of the house, stamping on the ground and poking it with spiky things. After half an hour they still had not found it so they asked if I had the plans to the house. I didn't know that either so it was decided I'd call Monsieur Fevrier the constructor. He said he would come and show the farm workers where it was and shortly after the mayor himself turned up wondering what had become of his workers. Monsieur Fevrier arrived and he too paced up and down suggesting where the farm workers should stick their spiky things next, until eventually it was found. The two farm workers started to dig whilst the mayor, Monsieur Fevrier, Lorraine, Tom and I looked on. In the meantime another of the mayor's workers had arrived and Phillipe the farmer from over the road pitched up too to see if he could help. This was getting a bit embarrassing, all these men here to look at the contents of our fosse tank. When the lid was finally located and removed by one of the men, I suddenly didn't want to be there. Having removed the lid exposing the unpleasant contents, he started to grumble about something. Taking his glove off and scratching his head, he beckoned to his colleagues, still with cigarettes sticking out of their mouths, who came and looked down the hole, muttered back to him and scratched their heads. Then one went to the tractor and putting on a pair of thick rubber gloves which reached up to his armpits he bent down over the hole while the other men stood round straining their necks to see what was going to come out. 'Oh my God', a huge ball of sanitary towels that had been bound together with the sticky bits you pulled off the back to stick it to the crutch of your knickers. The poor man was having to pull this enormous ball of used soggy sanitary towels, bound together with sticky strips, from the hole, tearing it apart as he did so whilst the other two men put the untangled mess into bin liners. I was hoping they weren't going to give it back to me and when I turned round to ask Lorraine what she thought she had gone and I quickly followed her. We hid in the house until the job was complete and the onlookers had dispersed.

The Channel Tunnel job had completed and as husband was now working expanding the M25 he rarely came home. When he came home for a weekend I was hoping he would do something outside to improve the garden. We did have a lawn at the front and a flower bed prepared on the left but no flowers in it. There was still no fence at the bottom of the back garden but I had planted a row of Leylandii across the front garden to provide some privacy. He did come home but worked on his car and then returned to England, saying he'd be home for three weeks at Christmas.

Chapter 3 - New Prospects

One weekend we decided to go to Canterbury to buy some good old English food that was unavailable in France. As we strolled down the main shopping road we came across a shop called The Third Eye, full of boot-leg T-shirts. Tom loved it. We got chatting to the owner, telling him we lived in France and how lovely it was apart from employment, and he suggested that we sell his T-shirts on the French markets. What a good idea, we thought. All we needed was £500 to buy some stock. The T-shirts were nice and Tom knew all the bands. There were a few with cannabis leaves on with funny slogans. We said we would come back at a later date and buy the stock we needed. The only person who would lend us that much money was husband, and it wouldn't hurt him to do that, we thought! After a lot of convincing that we would be making loads of money he reluctantly agreed to let us have it.

Next we checked out the local market, which we visited. It was held in Boulogne on Place Dalton every Wednesday and Saturday. I had to get a Carte de Commerce and then we needed tables and covers and an umbrella; we already had a garden umbrella in the garage. I was told that to get a place I would have to turn up at 7 in the morning and wait for the placier who would allocate a space for us.

Winter was already upon us and it was cold, so standing in a freezing cold market wasn't very appealing to me but needs must. We went back to Canterbury with our £500 and Tom picked out the T-shirts he thought would sell and we also got some patches and bandanas and other bits and pieces.

On Saturday 4th. December 1993. I woke up a businesswoman. I had my 'Carte de Commerce', £500 worth of credited boot-leg T-shirts, patches, badges, bandanas and woolly hats, a flimsy pasting table and an enormous garden umbrella inserted into a tiny disproportionate concrete foot. Tom and I were going off to Boulogne market and I did not have a clue how to run a business.

And here we were at 7 o'clock on a freezing windy December morning waiting for the guy in charge known as the 'placier' to allocate us our 2 metre space. Whilst we were waiting I gazed at the other stalls which consisted of vegetables, flowers, homemade honey, bread, cheeses, live rabbits squashed into tiny cages, live pigeons packed like sardines, plucked chickens laid out in rows with their necks and heads still attached. Not a place for animal rights activists to frequent! The placier eventually showed up at 8 o'clock and showed us our place which just happened to be right in front of the men's toilets. Then I was asked by another stall holder to move my car. Although it appeared to me that most of the marketeers had huge white vans parked next to their spaces, I kept being told to move it, but there was nowhere to move it to. The second problem was the ground was cobbled and so our table was constantly wobbling which was very annoying. We started to put our stuff out on the tables, and the umbrella in its stupid little stand, which wasn't going to last for more than 5 minutes. Tom started to arrange the T-shirts on the table. He put the ones with the goriest designs on them at the front - well known Rock Bands such as Goatwhore, Bad Religion, Morbid Angel, Death Anthrax and Slayer to name a few. There was a continuous flow of irritating men pushing past the end of our wobbling table in need of the toilet. I had noticed that the man on the stall next to us had erected something like a tablecloth to the side of his stall blocking himself from our view, so out of curiosity I walked round to the front to see what he was selling. How unattractive his stall was; just a few books. The man was not at all friendly and when I took a closer look at his wares, I realised that all his books were the same - they were bibles.

By the time we had finished with our display the weather had become more turbulent and things were beginning to fly off our table, which amused our French neighbours as they had all the right gear and nice big umbrellas, with huge heavy concrete weights holding nicely together, but their stuff was going nowhere. A mighty blast of wind in our direction blew the umbrella inside out and lifted all our display up and away, patches were blown nearly to the top of the church and landed several feet away from our stall so as fast that as we were gathering it up other stuff was blown away, not to mention becoming filthier by the minute. I guess our neighbour had sent the wrath of God in our direction. Chasing after our goods kept us occupied and warm whilst we waited and waited for our first customer who turned up at 11 o' clock and just happened to be

English ... and we were off, and by 12.30 we had 590 francs in our tin and had also been given orders for certain T-shirts. Midday the market was over and we packed up our dirty stock and went home, tired out.

I was impressed by our first day's takings but had learnt that marketplaces are cold and windy, umbrellas easily blow inside out and everything needs to be anchored down. The plan was to acquire the proper equipment so we would be in-keeping with other French market folk and not sticking out like English idiots to be ridiculed.

So from now on it was onwards and upwards.

Christmas was fast approaching, and we had been told that every year the Mayor of Wimereux, which was 5 kilometres down the coast, held a Christmas indoor market at the Hotel de Ville which was the mayor's office building. I went off to book us a place where I learnt that the Christmas market was on for a week and we could leave our stuff for the duration as there were going to be security guards patrolling the building throughout the night. It was decided that we would attend Boulogne market in the morning and when we had packed up we would go directly to Wimereux.

We packed up all the stuff when the market finished in Boulogne, having spent yet another cold and windy morning with rain clouds threatening. Anyway we had got through the morning dry but freezing. Arriving at Wimereux I went to the office to find where our pitch was located. There was a plan stuck on the wall and I found where we were going to be and asked where I should go next. I was told to go to the car park. We did that and when we got there we beheld a huge marquee erected there, covering the entirety of the car park by the Hotel de Ville, directly on the seafront. I thought we were going to be inside in the warm! Nothing was ever as I imagined it was going to be, it was always worse.

We lugged our stuff in and having just packed it all up started to unpack it all again. There were still lots of stall holders to turn up as the place was pretty empty, but opposite us were two Parisian gentlemen selling chocolates. We assembled our stall and then went home. The market was going to start the next day at 9 o'clock. The next day was very wet and very windy but despite the fact that there was only going to be a bit of canvas separating us from the raging storm we arrived early full of hope and great expectations of making a fortune. There were many more stalls than yesterday which was encouraging, and the two Parisians were already there sitting behind boxes of delicious chocolates. We politely acknowledged them and sat ourselves down behind our stall as the storm raged on outside. The marquee's walls and roof were being battered by the strong wind, so much so that it looked as though it would be uprooted from whatever was holding it down, which was quite scary, not to mention the rain that had begun to seep in at the edges, and if that wasn't enough it was so cold we could see our breath. Of course no normal person was going to venture out in such weather and so we sat there bored, waiting and terrorised by the banging and crashing of the marquee that surrounded us.

A few people had begun to trickle through and slowly but surely we made a few sales. The two Parisians decided that some entertainment was needed, so they attached a 50 franc note to a piece of string and placed it in the walk-way; every time someone stooped to pick it up they whisked it away. It was so funny and gave us a good laugh. By the time we got to day 3 we were up to our ankles in rainwater and had hardly sold anything. The weather was still turbulent and the Parisians were still playing tricks. By the end of the week we had only taken 1600 francs and by the time we had paid for the pitch it had not been worth the effort, so we went home wondering what it had all been about.

Lorraine having given up the Lycée in Boulogne and had undertaken a correspondence course to continue to get the A-levels she had started in England. She did the course in eight months and won her place at Roehampton Institute in London, and she went back to England in September 93 to start her 5-year degree.

Christmas was uneventful. Lorraine came home and so did husband; he spent most of the time in the garage, and Lorraine pottered about in her bedroom, while Tom and I looked for new markets to go to in the area for next year.

By March I was doing 5 markets a week. Tom came with me at the weekends, and we had bought two very old faded parasols and four lumps of concrete to act as weights to hold everything down.

We had discovered suppliers of other things in the UK so we decided to buy some just to see if they would be popular. We bought some very pretty pipes with old wizards and old long-haired men for the bowl, long plastic tubes with metal spouts known as bongs, and extra-long cigarette papers. We added more T-shirts to our stock - some had cannabis leaves on them, one had a picture of Pope John Paul 2nd. with a joint in his hand and written above it was: 'I like the Pope he Smokes Dope'. Another one was a drawing of a Rasta mowing a lawn and it said, 'Don't walk on the grass, smoke it'. We also purchased patches of bands and cannabis leaves. Some said, 'Smoke pot'. So with our new stock we set about getting back to the markets.

Tom's band was doing very well and they were playing lots of gigs in the area and wherever they played he would leave a pile of our leaflets advertising where we were going to be next. There was a fan club for Malice in Wonderland and the fans and fanettes would come to the markets and buy our stuff, just because the drummer of Malice in Wonderland was there.

There was one huge anxiety owning a business in France and that was the charges I had to pay. There was private health insurance, social security, and a retirement pension, and all had to be paid before you could start trading. Then, if that wasn't bad enough, VAT applied at the rate of 20% if your turnover was more than 70.000 francs a year. It amounted to hundreds of pounds which I didn't have so I asked if I could pay monthly till I got established and was told I could.

Chapter 4 - In Hot Pursuit

At last spring 1994 had blossomed and the warmer weather was here, which certainly made market days more pleasant, although the dilemma of where I could or could not park my car continued. I found these old Frenchmen tiresome and of course it was always the same ones, as they also did the same circuit of weekly markets as we did. It was OK for them to park their huge transit vans next to their stalls but they would not let me. Even if there was a space for my mine I was told to move it so one of them could park there. Eventually I was confident enough with my French to argue back to them but with little success. Sometimes it worked, but most times not. I had exchanged my car for a Citroen C15 van, much needed to transport all our stuff, especially with the umbrellas being quite long. One day at Etaple market I had been told yet again to move my van and I was so angry I slammed shut the back doors and, getting into the driver's seat, I revved up the engine to create a stink of fumes and drove off at speed, only to have to slam the brakes on hard immediately as I had trapped the edge of the canopy in the back doors - so when I raced off I had not only taken the umbrella and weights but the entire table had gone flying, scattering everything on it in random directions. Tom stood there stunned at seeing the beautiful display he had just spent an hour arranging scattered all over the road. It was the fault of these bloody Frenchmen. Well, that gave them a good laugh. I helped Tom retrieve all the stuff and reassemble the tables and umbrella, after which I drove off more cautiously to find a parking space, ignoring the mocking spectators.

Tom announced on his 15th birthday that he had quit school. I asked him if he was absolutely sure that's what he wanted, and he assured me it was because he could put the time into his drumming. Thank God for that, he wasn't learning anything anyway. I was totally happy with his decision, and it meant he could help me on the markets too.

We had also discovered brocantes and braderies which were held on Sundays in villages and towns, so every weekend there was always somewhere to go.

One particular Sunday we went to a town called Aire sur la Lys. It was a pretty town and the braderie was enormous, it expanded from the large 'place' - the town square - down several side streets to a smaller place, then continued down more side streets to a third place. It was the largest braderie we had been to so far and must have been popular by the number of stalls which were there. The streets were all cobbled with lots of cafés with chairs and tables outside which seemed to spill over onto the goods being sold by the 'brocanteurs', the sellers who if they were only selling bric-a-brac just laid a large piece of plastic on the ground and displayed their goods and chattels upon it. In the main square there was a four sided clock which had the longest sequence of chimes I had ever heard, about three minutes worth, and no sooner had it finished its hourly chiming than it chimed again every quarter of the hour.

Tom had a walkabout looking at the other stalls and got chatting to a young couple who were selling posters. They told us of a three-day braderie which was held in Lille and took place on the first weekend in September. They said it was hard work but you could make loads of money. We had a good day at the braderie in Aire sur la Lys and made some new friends.

The van had not been running properly and after a few weeks it broke down and was back in the garage where it had been purchased so it was back to the previous car, a Renault 18 which I had bought from an English friend for £50. I told the man at the garage I would need the van back by Friday night which gave him three days to repair it. Typical French, he said it would be ready and of course it wasn't so we had to pack the Renault with all the market stuff - umbrellas and all.

We had decided that this Saturday we would go to the market in Le Touquet for a change. We set off at 7.15. It was a lovely sunny day in May as we drove down the lane and passed the Château in Pittefaux, and as we were approaching the junction by the Hypermarket Auchan there, parked on the middle of the roundabout, was a Renault 5 with three douanes (customs officers) inside, two men and a woman.

We drove past them, but I checked the mirror a couple of times and suspected they were following us. Although the Renault had English number plates I was concerned as the tax disc was two years out of date and there was no MOT or insurance. To be certain they were following us I kept slowing down and then speeding up again and sure enough they did the same. I told Tom to stick the tax disc down his sock. Then after a few kilometres they shot past us and the woman was hanging out of the window waving her arm about indicating for us to pull in. I was cursing that damn man from the garage; the van was all legal and now here we were with the Renault that was totally illegal and what's more we would lose a place at the Le Touquet market.

So there we were parked on the side of the road! All three got out of their car and proceeded to walk round ours. One of the men started kicking the wheels and bumper. Then the woman told me to open the window which I did but only slightly. She asked me for my papers. Now when in France you are expected to carry all your documents with you including your passport, everything appertaining to your vehicle and permits to work etc. I slipped my 'Carte de Commerce' and my 'Carte de Sejour' through the narrow gap at the top of the window, but oh my days she wanted the documents for the car. I am not a good liar on the spur of the moment but I said the car belonged to my husband and he had all the papers with him in Belgium, pleased with myself for the quick thinking.

Next she wanted to know where we were going and what was in the back of the car and then she demanded all the invoices for our entire stock. Who in God's name drives around with a pile of invoices? So we were told we had to follow them back to Saint Martin de Boulogne to the douanes office, which meant we had no chance of getting to the market in Le Touquet.

When we arrived Tom was led off in one direction and me in another. They asked me where I had bought the stock, and the woman even knew where our place was in Boulogne Market which meant they had been spying on us. What on earth did they think we were doing? I had to show all my papers, but most of them were at home. In the meantime Tom was being questioned if he had ever seen drugs or been offered any, and they searched his pockets.

I was led outside by two men to the car and ordered to open the back, where they proceeded to rummage through all our stuff. One pulled a pair of jams out of a box which were long shorts to the calf. He asked me how much they were, so I asked him if he wanted to buy them. He held them against himself and said they weren't his style. Then a Labrador was brought out and shoved in the car, he was a cream coloured dog and I was worried he would cover everything in dog hair as most of our T-shirts and jams were black. I asked the douanier what he was looking for and he replied 'nothing, we're just giving him some exercise' so I retorted that in England we walk our dogs, it's good for the owners as well. After that we were free to go, but I had to return in the afternoon with the invoices for the stock and the car would have to be registered in France and have a French number plate. 'Yeah like hell' I thought.

So after that little episode we drove into Boulogne to try and get a place in the market, which we did. I guessed that someone had reported that we were selling drugs just because we had a few T-shirts with cannabis leaves on them.

We thought that someone had grassed on us to the douanes. There were a couple of Moroccan men, we called Rock Marok and Squat Morok. Rock Marok was tall and thin and Squat Marok was short and fat. They sold similar things to us but their T-shirts had faces of lions and dogs on them and they sold flags of Michael Jackson, Johnny Halliday and other unpopular people. Ours were much better, and better quality too, of popular rock bands and cannabis leaves and the middle finger 'up yours'. Or could it have been our bible bashing neighbour who had condemned me to hell for selling a T-shirt with the Pope smoking a joint, which he said was sacrilegious, as if I was bothered!

I returned to the douane office in the afternoon with the papers they had demanded, and each invoice was photocopied in triplicate. The French are obsessed with paper and must be guilty of the most unnecessary deforestation in the world. So I guessed that I was now under suspicion of being a drug dealer. I had smoked pot in 1969, when I had been a hippie for a summer. There were 7 of us living in a one-bedroom basement flat in Warrior Square in Hastings and only one person going out to work to pay the rent. I walked everywhere in bare feet and ended up with a verruca, happy days they were too!

Well, it was up to them; if they wanted to waste their time waiting to catch me selling drugs they were in for a long wait.

The following Monday I had to go to Boulogne and then go to the garage to see the man about the van. I left home, and when I got to the bottom of the hill at Pittefaux there by the Château gates was a parked Peugeot 106 with a guy sitting in it wearing a leather jacket and sunglasses. I glanced at him as I drove past and thought he looked like one of those plain clothes police spies you see in films. Anyway I thought no more of him and carried on to Boulogne. Driving past Auchan I looked in the mirror and noticed the spy guy was behind me. Surely I wasn't being followed again! But I was and he followed me all the way to Boulogne. When I arrived in the town I quickly parked the car and purposely walked down the no entrance way to a one-way street so he couldn't follow. During the hour I spent in Boulogne the spy guy passed me four times in his car and each time I glared at him to let him know I knew he was following me.

After Boulogne I went on to Colembert to see the man at the garage about the van. It was fixed and he said he would deliver it that afternoon which he did. So we transferred the market stuff back to the van ready for the market in Etaples the following day.

Chapter 5 - The Heavies Arrive

The next day was Tuesday, and we went to Le Touquet as we had missed it on Saturday thanks to those douaniers. It was a lovely sunny day and I was hoping to do well. We set up and started selling almost immediately, then at around 10.30 two policemen pitched up and began to examine our goods closely. One was looking at the T-shirts on the rack, pulling them out one by one, checking the fronts and then the backs whilst the other one was picking up stuff off the table. We had a basket full of badges mostly of pop stars and groups, some with cannabis leaves and some with 'Piss Off' and 'Fuck Off'. He picked out the badge with 'Fuck Off' written on it and asked in English 'what means fook off?' 'to tell someone to go away' I replied 'do you want to buy it?' He put it back and picked out another one. 'What means pees off?' he asked. 'To tell someone to go away', I replied. Then he picked one with a cannabis leaf on it and pointing to it he said sternly, 'Interdit' (forbidden). He continued, pointing to the pipes, bongs, postcards and patches, everything with a cannabis leaf on or related to smoking it, saying, 'Interdit' every time. 'Code Penal 630'. 'Why is it Interdit?' I asked him, but he didn't answer and off they strolled. That was the third time we had been followed, stopped and visited in less than a week. Surely that would be it now and they will give up pursuing us.

So our lives carried on hassle free for a month.

Early one evening in June we needed to go to Auchan, and as we got into the van I noticed three men driving past our house too slowly staring at us. 'What are you staring at?' I shouted at them, but they didn't say why. We drove off, only to pass them a few hundred metres up the road where they had pulled in. So instead of taking the lane to Pittfaux I turned right into the lane to Hesdin and blow me down they followed us, but, having made a slight detour with them close behind, when we turned left to go to Auchan they turned right in the direction of Wimereaux. Who the hell were they? Surely they couldn't still be the douaniers? After that I used to get a strange feeling that I was being watched, but undeterred I lost no sleep over it and we carried on regardless.

Next we went to St. Omer for a braderie, the first Sunday in June. I was a bit disappointed as it was not as big as I had imagined it would be. It was not even on the place, instead it was down a narrow side street. The weather forecast wasn't too great either, sunny in the morning and raining in the afternoon, and it wasn't very warm either.

We set up the stall as usual, but for some strange reason Tom had displayed all the druggie T-shirts in the front. We had some new ones now, 'The Daily Leaf', 'The Sunday Joint' and 'Legalise Cannabis'. I told him he was rather silly doing that after all the hassle we had had, but he said it was ok and I did change them but he put them back again. St. Omer must have had the highest population of cannabis smokers in the Pas-de-Calais region. The pipes, cigarette papers and cannabis T-shirts were selling like hot cakes and we were making mega bucks - well to our standard anything over 1000 francs was mega-bucks.

At 11.30 two fat, butchy middle aged women plodded past our stall and stopped. I had a feeling they were plain clothes policewomen. One told Tom that the T-shirts were interdit and we had no right to display them and certainly must not sell them. Tom retorted quite rudely that we were allowed to sell them and they didn't know what they were talking about. I quietly told him to shut up as the two women pointed at the pipes and papers, mumbling and tutting. Eventually they waddled off into the crowd, and I noticed they both had swollen feet bulging over their unsuitable shoes.

The weather forecast had been right and by the afternoon it had started raining and had turned colder. Then, sure enough, at 2 o'clock two policemen appeared just as I was selling a Daily Leaf t-shirt. One of the policemen snatched it out of my hands as I was carefully folding it. How dare he? I glared at him. I was furious, as someone had just paid for that. So here we go again same old routine everything is interdit and the occasional Code Penal 630L was mentioned. 'Excuse me', I said in my best French to the copper, we are in Europe and I purchased these T-shirts in England and paid VAT on them, so why should they be legal over there and illegal here. I put my hand out for the copper to return the t-shirt which he did...The commotion had gathered quite a crowd and I had whispered to the customer to wait till they had gone and I would let him have his t-shirt. Before the policemen left they told me to put everything into my van which luckily I had been able to park by us that day. They asked for my papers, passport, invoices, carte de commerce etc. name and address and so on. They left and we then sold all the druggie stuff to the crowd of onlookers from the back of the van. At the end of the day we had taken 3000 francs thanks to the police of St. Omer.

I had been dreading the thought of spending the winter standing in freezing cold markets again. The summer markets were fun, plenty of customers and you got a tan as well. That is when I thought about opening a shop in Boulogne. No more hanging around in the cold and wet but inside in the warm instead and no more complaints about where I parked the van. It seemed like the way forward.

Since we had not seen husband since Christmas I had learnt to change the wheels on the van myself. I had performed this operation twice successfully. The first time I had jacked it up and attached the wheel brace and jumped vigorously on it to loosen the first nut but it wouldn't undo so I kept jumping until someone told me I was doing it up, not undoing it! So I started to jump in the opposite direction and it did undo and so did the other 3, job done. Now it needed new brake pads. They really didn't work and made a fearful grating noise, even if I wasn't applying the brakes, so I decided if I could change a wheel, I could change the brake pads. I had to do all my car repairs in a public car park in case I got stuck and had to ask a man for help. So I bought a pair of brake pads and jacked the van up, removed the wheel and then as I took each part off I laid it in an orderly line so I would know which bit went on next. The first one was easy, and I put everything back, then went to the other one did the same procedure as the other side but hit a snag when I got to removing the old brake pad. It had worn so thin it had welded to the wheel and it was impossible to remove it. I put everything back, but the problem now was when I applied the brakes the van swerved to the right. I suppose one brake was better than no brakes.

Chapter 6 - A Trip to Hastings

Tom's band had been doing really well and was very popular in the area. They had just organised a small tour in England, a concert in Canterbury and 3 in Hastings. I wanted to go and see one of their concerts so it was decided I would go to the last one and I would take a few fans with me. One of the artistic fanettes made the words Malice in Wonderland and stuck them on both sides of the van, and also painted playing cards here and there and the odd cannabis leaf; it looked wonderful. I looked forward to going to Hastings to see Tom playing but so did the 14 fans who had asked to come with me. How was I going to fit 14 teenagers into my two-seater van and be able to drive it safely plus the problem with the brakes which I had tried to repair? I had learnt how to stop by applying a quick gear change and at the right moment yank on the hand brake. In this way I could usually stop before I got to the junction. Being responsible for all these young lives was worrying, so I contacted a friend and asked her if she could meet us in Dover in her Espace and ferry the overspill to Hastings, to which she agreed thankfully. I also contacted another friend who was going to sort the brake problem out.

The band set off late one night after performing a concert in Boulogne. Their first concert was to be in Canterbury followed by three in Hastings with one night free before their last concert on the Wednesday in a pub called The Crypt.

At six thirty in the morning on day four of the UK tour I was awoken by the phone ringing. I rushed downstairs in a panic wondering what on earth had happened, and it was Tom. He explained; the previous evening they had decided to go for a drink after which they went for a drive along Hastings sea front to St. Leonards. Xavier the roadie had decided to climb out of the van window whilst the van was moving. He had managed to get his whole body outside and stand on the open window frame whilst hanging on to the top of the window. All of a sudden Rab slammed the brakes on which had caused Xavier to loosen his grip and he was tossed onto the road breaking his arm. Next stop was the Conquest Hospital where they spent several hours for Xavier to have his broken arm set in plaster of Paris. They were on their way again and once in the town Rab inadvertently drove through a red light directly in front of a stationary police car. As they drove on the police car followed and in turn stopped them and Rab was breathalysed with a positive result. The others were made to get out of the van and were questioned. Tom said he pretended to be French and said his name was Antoine Le Blanc and pretended he couldn't speak English. So as Tom was being questioned in English he was answering in French which blew his cover and the policeman realised this non-speaking English boy could understand perfectly well what he was being asked.

The band was staying with my friends in Bexhill and Arno took over the driving. I rang Hastings police to find out Rab's fate. I was told that he had been breathalysed and was found to be over the legal limit, and also that they had found cannabis in the vehicle but not very much. Consequently Rab was banned from driving for eighteen months and received a hefty £500 fine. The ban only applied in England so he would be able to drive in France although he didn't own a car. So he was released from police custody in time for the final concert.

Everyone who was going to the Malice concert stayed in our house the night before. I allocated 15 minutes of bathroom time to each of the girls, and then 10 minutes to the boys providing they went in in pairs, but even then we had to get up three hours before we were due to leave. Then there was the big problem of getting everyone into the van, largest first and the smaller ones to sit on top of the boys, then three in front, one on a lap the other on the gear stick. Crushed is an understatement, there was a considerable lack of breathing space too, but Calais was only half an hour up the road.

We set off with great care. I felt uneasy with the lack of brakes and made several wishes; one that I wouldn't have to do an emergency stop, two that we didn't meet any gendarmes or police en route and three that none of my passengers had brought any illegal substances with them. Greatly relieved we arrived unscathed at Calais Port. I deposited the overspill of my passengers at the entrance for foot-passengers and the three of us carried on to the vehicle departure gate.

The crossing went smoothly and we disembarked in the same fashion we had boarded. Maggie was there waiting for us and took charge of her passengers, Natalie who we had met at Aire sur La Lys had come with her friend Patty and we sang Milord by Edith Piaf all the way to Hastings where I dropped them off, then I drove straight to my friend to get the brakes repaired.

The evening of the much-awaited Malice in Wonderland concert was amazing, the pub was packed and they did a great show. Lots of my friends had turned up too but disappointingly chose to sit round the edge of the dance floor in the quieter shadows rather than be up at the front with me head-banging with all the young people. I always joined in, even when the raving reached fever pitch and everybody's purpose was to bump into each other with the intention to knock over or out as many revellers as possible. I loved it, anyway what else were you meant to be doing at 44 when all your friends were teenagers?

Lorraine had managed to be there to see her brother and we had also brought her current boyfriend with us. He was a bit strange and claimed to have slept in a coffin with his dead mother for a week! I had noticed that Tom was drinking quite a lot of lager during the course of the evening and he was becoming a bit intoxicated so I suggested he didn't have any more.

The evening came to an end and we had all enjoyed ourselves, but it was very late and we had the journey back to Dover ahead of us. The group van was packed up with the band's gear and the fans and fanettes decided who was going in which vehicle. Arno had taken over the driving as Rab had been banned. Everybody wanted to go in the group van so Natalie and Patty came with me. The plan was I would follow on behind.

It was 3 a.m. by the time we set off, and I was beginning to feel tired and not looking forward to the journey to Dover. We got as far as Rye and all of a sudden the van pulled in and everyone started to jump out of the side door and were running amok all over the road with their hands over their faces. Natalie, Patty and I pulled in behind and watched in amazement at what appeared to be mass hysteria. The only person I couldn't account for was Tom who, it transpired, had been the cause of the chaos, having vomited all over the occupants and all the group's bedding as well. So when calm was restored it was decided Tom would swap places with Natalie. We set off again, and after a few miles the van pulled in again, the door slid open and out jumped Natalie also vomiting, caused by the smell of Tom's vomit.

The remainder of the journey passed without interruption and we got the ferry back to Calais. After I had delivered everybody safely to their homes and no doubt their anxious parents, I eventually got into bed at 10 a.m. shattered.

Chapter 7 - The Augmentation

Early evening of Rockstock 1 in the back garden

At the beginning of August 1994 I decided it was time to look for a shop, and going on the information Natalie had given us of the potential mega bucks we were hoping to earn at Lille Braderie it would be enough to pay for a deposit, rent, agents' fees and lots of stock. Excited and full of enthusiasm I walked round Boulogne to see what was on offer, a shop right in the town centre would have been ideal. There were a few on Grand Rue and Rue de Faidherbe the two main shopping areas, but with a high rent. But just off Grand Rue I had seen an empty shop on Rue National where there were three schools and two colleges in the vicinity.

I made a rendezvous with the agent, a Monsieur Prudhomme. He was a flamboyant character, a tall man in his thirties, with a huge moustache like two turned up bananas under his nose and a mop of brown curly hair. His eyebrows rose and fell as he spoke. Sadly his taste in fashion was rather outdated, back to the 1940's I'd say, he was wearing a mustard coloured shirt, adorned by a bright green and blue paisley tie, a brown and yellow tartan jacket, green trousers, brown lace up shoes and a beige flasher mac. The most charming gentleman I had ever met, and when he said hello or good-bye he would take my hand and make a little bow.

I accompanied him to the shop in Rue National, and we entered via a back door. The shop was a decent size, about 40 square metres, with fitted carpet and two counters, one with a glass top and display shelf underneath and space for a till. There was a toilet and a small cupboard for surplus stock. The window at the front of the shop was large, and there was a double glass door to the entrance with an electric metal shutter. Unfortunately the previous tenant had sold perfume and the walls were painted a horrible dull pink. I imagined how the shop would look once it had been decorated and so I agreed there and then I would take it. The rent was reasonable, 2800 francs per month, and I said we would open on the 1st. October and I would like two weeks rent free to prepare the shop for decorating and install railings etc. Monsieur Prudhomme agreed to my request, then promptly announced he would like his fee now of 3000 francs. I would have to pay one month's rent in advance and a month's rent as a deposit. I said that would be fine, hoping upon hope that Natalie was right in her forecast for the Lille Braderie. I think I had given Monsieur Prudhomme the impression I had plenty of money and he was full of enthusiasm to get our shop up and running.

As I walked back to the van I was excited to start this new venture. I've always been impulsive and didn't ever concern myself whether it was a good idea or not. At this moment in time it seemed like a good idea.

August 1994 was the 25th anniversary of Woodstock, an American music festival that had been held between August 15th - 19th 1969, and had attracted an audience of 400,000. It had been billed as 'An Aquarian Exposition: 3 Days of Love and Peace', and it was held on 600-acre dairy farm 43 miles south west of Woodstock. It had been an amazing festival with top artists like Jimi Hendrix, Joe Cocker, Janice Joplin, The Who, Mott the Hoople and many more, and it had inspired me to become a pot-smoking, peace loving hippie for a time.

Coming up was Lorraine's 21st birthday so I had the ambitious idea of having our own Woodstock and celebrating Lorraine's birthday at the same time, but maybe not on such a grand scale as

Woodstock. We knew plenty of bands and most of the young people in Boulogne. We found four local bands all eager to play at our 'Rockstock' as I named it. Malice in Wonderland, The Backwards, Clever Cloud and Sober Cow. I would not be able to supply everyone with food and drink, so I invited the pizza man whom I'd met at Etaples market to come to Rockstock to sell his pizza's. As for drinks people would have to bring their own. We made fliers and handed them out at the markets and on the streets of Boulogne. Phillipe the farmer, our neighbour who lived directly opposite us, provided some very large sheets of chipboard to construct a flat stage in the back garden.

A week before the event to be held on the 27th I allocated the job to Lorraine and Emilie, Tom's girlfriend, to call on the residents in the commune Le Trou D'enfer and warn them of what was going to occur the following weekend, which they duly did with apparently no hostility from anyone. Most said they would go away for the weekend.

As we lived out in the country it may have been difficult for festival goers to find us, but as luck would have it there was a band from somewhere else doing a concert at the CJC Leon Blum Recreation Centre in Boulogne a week before Rockstock and they had put wooden panels advertising it all over Boulogne. I had an idea, if we waited till the time they were actually performing I could go out in the van and nick all their panels on legs as they'd be long gone before we would be putting them back again.

After a deluge of rain in the morning there was a lot of activity going on in the garden by the time I got home from the market. The stage was laid out in the corner of the garden which they had managed to elevate about 2 inches and it was level enough to be able to stand speakers, microphones and drum kits on. There were metres of extension cables all leading to various sockets in the house by way of the kitchen window and there were as many sound technicians as there were electricians. The lighting had been cleverly arranged including one spotlight being attached to the top of the rotating washing line, some hanging off gutter pipes and others balanced precariously on the branches of the neighbours' trees.

As soon as I got home I unpacked the van of market stuff and reloaded it with all the stolen panels I had taken the previous weekend, which were now displaying nice fresh signs to Rockstock and an appropriate directional arrow. So off I went to re-establish the signs in the same holes as I had removed them from making sure the arrows were facing in the right direction.

When I got back the pizza man had arrived but was looking perturbed because he couldn't get his van up the driveway as it was too steep, so I suggested that instead he could leave it at the bottom of the driveway on the side of the road with a couple of traffic cones for safety which I had acquired from somewhere.

Phillipe had said that we could use his long driveway as a car park and people had started to arrive. During the next hour I had a few glasses of Pastis - not a great idea as I hadn't eaten anything, since I had been busy doing other things. I had bought 8 cases of beer for the helpers and a bottle of Pastis for anyone who might fancy it.

The crowds had gathered

People started to arrive and Phillipe's long driveway was filling up with cars fast and by eight o'clock both the toilets were broken. I was in the kitchen socialising with some of Tom's friends, telling stories of when I had become a hippy in the summer of 69 when there had been seven of us all living in a basement flat in Warrior Square, St. Leonards-on-Sea. One of the guys went out to work to pay the rent, one attended Hastings Art College while the rest of us did nothing but wander around Hastings every day in bare feet. There was a bakery nearby and Gillie and I used to go there at 4 in the morning begging for bread and we were always given a couple of freshly baked crusty loaves and in the evenings we would have other hippy friends round and we'd all sit crossed legged in a circle passing joints round and listening to Van Morrison's Madame George or Astral Weeks till we were stoned. We were so Peace and Love, happy, without a care in the world. Whilst I was recounting my youth I was handed a joint which I accepted, and took a puff for old times' sake, in turn passed it on to the next person and within seconds I was handed another and another and another, it was like being back in that basement flat in Warrior Square.

I hadn't been hungry earlier but after all that pot-smoking I now had the munches, so I went off to find the pizza man. I joined the queue and was happy to see that he had so many customers, but as it got to my turn and as I was ordering my pizza I came over strange and fell backwards, and the next thing I knew I was spread-eagled on the driveway unable to move a limb, though my brain was still working and I could think. I thought it must have been the cocktail of pastis and cannabis which had caused this unfortunate situation and how funny it would be if I laid there and died in front of all these teenagers having just been boasting to them about my hippy pot smoking summer of 69.

Sadly for me Rockstock was over. I remember being carried and every time I was put down somewhere I vomited, occasionally regaining consciousness only to find myself somewhere different and again vomiting everywhere. I remembered Lorraine giving me a handful of carrier bags.

The next morning I felt as fit as a fiddle. First I needed to pee and going into the bathroom I noticed a man asleep in the bath, so I had to pee hoping he wouldn't wake up. Downstairs there were bodies everywhere. I stepped over them and looked into the garden and the mess was horrendous. But as people started to wake we all went into the garden with bin liners and cleared all the rubbish, and as the festival goers began to leave we tidied up the house and someone mended the toilets.

I was so sorry I'd missed Rockstock. Malice in Wonderland had learnt a medley of songs from Woodstock especially for me but sadly I missed them. However, the whole thing had been a great success and so next year we would make it bigger and better and I had my eye on Phillipe's field with the mountain of cow dung in the middle of it.

Sober Cow doing their gig

Chapter 8 - Lille Braderie

Apart from my regular suppliers of boot-leg T-shirts I had found another supplier in Hastings called Mason's Music where I could buy official T-shirts which were much better quality. They also sold flags, patches, post cards, jams and ski caps, so we stocked up well in preparation for the fast-approaching Lille Braderie.

I wasn't sure if I was looking forward to or dreading it. Natalie had told me that there would be loads of thieves so we should take plenty of helpers for serving and watching. Natalie said she would be there to help us.

The previous night we packed the van to the hilt; in fact it was worse than when I had taken the 14 fans to Hastings. We had boxes and large stripy laundry bags crammed with stock, weights to secure the parasols, three pasting tables, a clothing rack, hundreds of non-slip coat hangers which had attached themselves to each other in a bin liner, two stools, a deck chair and a hammock plus our bedding, pillows, a change of clothing and washing stuff. We put the parasols down the centre of the van, the tops of them resting on top of the dashboard and the other ends wedged in two holes which were located behind the rear lights of the van. We had great difficulty closing the rear doors.

I had commandeered Arno to come with us and because of our earlier departure he stayed the night. We had to get up at 2 o'clock, so there really was no point in going to bed but we did. Tom had to squash into the back of the van and Arno sat in the front.

Heading for the unknown at 5am we picked up Natalie, who had brought Patty along with her too. They lived in Lilliers, 32 kilometres south of Lille, and they were waiting for us. Patty climbed into the back of the van with Tom, Arno got out to let Natalie in and with great difficulty she ended up sitting astride the parasols. We were just about to leave when she asked me if I had brought any lighting with us and I hadn't so out she got again and reappeared with a thing that looked like a Triffid, a 2 metre long pole with a strange shaped light on the end, so that had to be put in the back of the van which upset Tom and Patty as they had just settled themselves again. I had no idea how the light would work as we

didn't have a generator. Natalie got back in the van, she put one foot
on the dashboard and the other amongst the foot pedals, and we set
off. I had great difficulty changing gear so Natalie tried to operate
the clutch, which sometimes worked and sometimes didn't. This was
the mother of all driving skills and I couldn't wait to get there to be
out of this uncomfortable and dangerous situation. There was one
bonus, at least I had brakes!

We had to arrive in Lille by 6.30 a.m. to ensure that we found and
then guarded our patch as there was no charge for a space at the
braderie and it was going to be every man for himself fighting for
the best places. The half hour journey ended abruptly when Natalie
led me down a one-way street the wrong way. There was no way I
could see to reverse out, so with Natalie one side of the road and
Arno the other and only wing mirrors to look at they guided me
safely out of the side street onto the main road we had just left.

There was hustle and bustle as far as the eye could see, with
police and CRS (Compagnie Républicaine de Sécurité) everywhere.
We headed straight for the 'Grand Place' which was the centre of the
braderie. The commerçants (traders) and white transit vans were
occupying every conceivable space and it was only 6 o'clock in the
morning.

We arrived at the Grand Place and there were bollards all the way
round it apart from one small space left for emergency services to
gain access if necessary and it was 'interdit' (forbidden) to private
vehicles, so ignoring the sign I drove through the gap onto the place.
We chose our space and I parked on it, the others got out of the van
and went off for a wander and left me alone. I wanted to have a sleep
as I was tired from getting up so early. I had started to nod off when
there was knocking on the window. I opened my weary eyes and saw
lots of blue uniforms peering in at me so I unwound the window and
saw 5 policemen.

I had to make a quick decision as to whether I was going to speak
in French or pretend to not understand depending on the reason for
their visit. Then one of them said I couldn't park where I was and I'd
have to move off the place, so decision made I looked at him and
raised my shoulders. I was not going to move the van for someone
else to take our place. I stared at him blankly and said 'I not
understand' in English trying to sound foreign, and to my annoyance

he damn well spoke English 'No car ere' he said. His colleagues were looking through the window trying to see what I had inside. I was hoping they wouldn't ask to see the stock in case they confiscated it. I smiled at the policeman and said I would move, they strolled off and one looked back over his shoulder then said something to his colleague who also turned his head in my direction.

We had to guard our patch for 11 hours until we were allowed to set up shop at 5 o'clock that afternoon and with already one encounter within 15 minutes of arriving I was pretty doubtful that we were going to last the duration. Finally I was able to get to sleep but two hours later there was another knock on the window, this time it was two different policemen telling me to move the van off the 'place'. I replied to him in French and said that I had never been to Lille before and if I moved off the Place I would get lost, smiling sweetly as I did so and to my delight he said I could stay but not to set up shop till 5pm. No sooner had he gone than I saw the 5 CRS men who had hassled me earlier, over they came but said nothing, but the biggest one took a book of parking tickets out of his back pocket and proceeded to write me a parking ticket. In the heat of the moment I had forgotten I'd said I didn't speak French and screamed at him that the other policeman had just said I could stay there. 'Oh, you do speak French' he said, 'Yes, but not when I'm tired' I replied. 'I told you to move your vehicle, but you are still here, so now I will give you an 'amende' (a parking fine.) ' But the other one said I could stay here' I winced. 'No you cannot' he replied 'Get off the place now or I will have your vehicle removed by the 'Dépanneuse', the breakdown truck' he threatened. I wasn't in the mood for this annoying man so I started the engine and moved the van about a foot, turned the engine off and said 'I've moved it', but seeing the menacing look on the policeman's face I thought better of it and reluctantly drove off. Then I saw Tom and the others and I told them to go and wait on our patch as I had to move the car off the place. When I got to the gap in the bollards there were several more policemen guarding the exit and they told me I would not be able to leave as there was a marathon just about to start. Why on earth would they arrange a marathon on the perimeter of the place when it was just about to be swamped with thousands of people?

So where was I to go? I drove slowly around, looking for somewhere I could get off the place; there were people and vehicles being evicted everywhere so a mass exodus was in full swing. I found a gap in the bollards and got onto the road and just opposite was a small street where some people had already set up their stalls and were doing a roaring trade. I just parked up at the entrance of the small street and made my way back to Tom and our patch, I was very worried that the van might be burgled. I found them all standing in a row watching the marathon which was running the periphery of the place. After five minutes of watching it I was bored just watching the same runners going round and round accompanied by motor cyclists, the pillion sitting back to front filming the event for television.

It was 11 o'clock by now and I was tired and bored so I decided to go back to the van and get the hammock so I could guard the space and sleep at the same time, and now it looked as if it was going to rain.

I struggled back with the hammock and assembled it and Natalie and Patty went to the van to have a nap, while Tom and Arno went off to explore. I closed my tired eyes and all I could hear was the clattering of feet and the clapping of hands as the runners ran round and round in ever decreasing circles. I couldn't sleep for all the noise but I did hang on to our patch. Later Tom took over the hammock and I went off to have something to eat and drink. I found a café on the place, which was clean and pleasant, all the waiters were wearing black trousers, white shirts, black bowties and black satin backed waist coats. Each one had a tray balanced on the palm of his hand. I sat at a table and ordered a 'chocolat chaud de maison' a hot chocolate. When it arrived I was given a very large empty cup on a saucer with a jug of hot milk and a large jug of melted chocolate, I poured both the milk and chocolate into the cup at the same time, oh my goodness it was the most delicious hot chocolate I had ever had in my life! I didn't want to leave a drop so I started to scrape the teaspoon round and round the jug that had the chocolate in. After I had finished I looked at the bill, bloody hell it was 20 francs that's nearly £2.50 but I guess worth every centime. Then I checked the toilets out which were clean and decided that this toilet would be my bathroom for the next three days. I left the café and went and bought a ham baguette. It was now 2 o'clock and we had only another 3 hours to wait. I got back to our patch and the marathon was still in full swing but many of the competitors were puffed out, fatigued, hot and sweating and dropping like flies.

Eventually the marathon came to an end and all of a sudden there was a rush of great activity going on around us as people started to set up their stalls so without another thought I rushed off to get the van, I carefully drove back weaving in and out of the already assembled stalls and the displays which were covering the ground.

As soon as I got back it was all hands-on deck, tables and parasols up, table covers on. Natalie and I hung the T-shirts on the rail and I had bought non slip hangers to prevent them being slipped off and stolen. Tom was doing the table display of pipes, metal badges, belt buckles, patches, bandana's, cigarette papers and bongs. The customers started arriving and buying before we had finished setting up so the first hour was total pandemonium. Arno, Tom and I were serving while Natalie and Patty kept watch for thieves. In less than an hour we had taken 1500 francs. We were selling like I'd ever known it before, there were thousands of people everywhere.

As it started to get dark I thought about Natalie's triffid in the van. There was a man selling jumpers just down from us and he had lights running off a generator so I went to ask him if we could plug the triffid in for 50 francs to which he kindly agreed, but then I realised that the cable on the triffid was nowhere near long enough to reach our patch so I had to ask the man if I could borrow his extension lead as well and he let us, so in no time we had light.

I should have been tired out but with the weight and sound of all that money in my black-market bag I was wide awake and full of energy. I wanted it to go on like this forever - mega bucks at long last and no visits from the police or douanes.

It was raining by 10 o'clock, drizzle sweeping sideways, but I didn't care. A woman had installed herself next to us with a table full of clay pipes which were selling like hot cakes. She was sitting behind her table smoking a large joint. I asked her if she had ever had problems with the police selling her clay pipes and she said she hadn't and besides they weren't illegal and she was surprised that I had. The poor woman had no parasol to keep herself and her pipes dry and she was soaking wet but she didn't appear to be bothered as I think she was too stoned.

We worked well into the night, the whole place was awash with people drinking and being rowdy and laughing. It looked like it would go on all night, the ground was becoming covered in empty beer bottles which were constantly being kicked and smashed by the crowds of people.

At 2 o'clock we decided to pack everything back into the van and get some sleep. We just left the tables one on top of the other and the parasols too. Arno, Patty and Natalie went off to stay with friends, while Tom climbed into the back of the van and I shut it after him. The stoned woman asked if she could sleep on the hammock as she didn't have a car, I felt so sorry for her to have to sleep outside in the rain with the drunken throng milling about. I left the hammock under the parasol for her. I bid her good night and thought what a state she looked; she had probably been quite beautiful in her younger days but too many years of smoking pot had taken their toll and her face was too wrinkled for her age and her thick blond grey unkempt hair was half up and the other half had fallen down. She was stoned and happy. I got in the van, wrapped my quilt around me, still wearing my black-market bag full of money, and dropped off to sleep.

I was awoken by the crashing of broken bottles. It was still dark and I looked outside, the stoned woman was lying on the hammock smoking yet another joint. She was directly in the line of drizzle so she had pegged a piece of plastic to the side of the parasol and was trying to shelter from the rain. Sadly her piece of plastic was too short and serving no purpose whatsoever. Instead of moving the hammock closer to the parasol she moved herself on the hammock, so when she went too far over she was tipping out of it. It was quite amusing to watch her and every time she fell out she struggled back in again muttering to herself and puffing on her soggy joint. I settled down again and all I could hear was bottles being smashed.

Not long after I woke again. The van was all steamed up and my legs were stiff and I wanted to stretch them. I wriggled about a bit and then opened the window, and what a surprise, there were three black men asleep under the parasol and they had made themselves a shelter with my tables. They had no covers and were using their bags of merchandise as pillows. The stoned woman had gone and there was a black man on the hammock. The guy looked at me and said 'Bonjour Madame'. I smiled at him and shut the window and felt thankful that I was lucky to be squashed in the van and not outside in the rain lying under a flimsy table.

The next time I woke up it was light, I opened the window and looked outside to see a new man asleep on the hammock and one left under the table, then the big clock on the square chimed 8 o'clock. I felt so dirty, I had been wearing the same clothes for over twenty-four hours and had not washed since yesterday morning. So I needed to get to the nice café as quickly as possible, I glanced at myself in the mirror and saw how dishevelled I was, put my Doc Martens on with great difficulty and gathered my wash bag and a change of clothing and put it all in a carrier bag. I arrived at the café and in fear of being thrown out if they realised that I had come there to use their facilities as a bathroom, I chose to sit at a table and indulge in another hot chocolate which I drank with great delight. As soon as I had finished my drink I shot off to the bathroom where I washed my face and cleaned my teeth then clutching my carrier bag and my baby wipes in the other I went into the toilet to finish off and get dressed, which was not easy as I had to hop about because I didn't want to put my bare feet on the toilet floor. You never could be sure what might be lurking there. So, dressed and clean, I quickly slapped on a bit of make-up and brushed my hair, and left the café feeling clean and ready for the day's onslaught.

Back at the van I woke Tom and sent him off to the café to get cleaned up and have some breakfast. Presently Arno, who had now been joined by his girlfriend Frede, Natalie and Patty arrived. Like the previous day we had non-stop selling. I didn't know if we had had anything stolen, but I expected we had, as even though we were now six it was still very difficult to keep an eye on everything. As we worked through the day Frede suddenly noticed that a buckle with an embossed cannabis leaf on it was missing which was worth 200 francs but there was nothing we could do.

That evening when it was starting to get dark I paid the man with the generator another 50 francs to plug the Triffid in. During the evening I caught some young people stuffing a T-shirt into a bag. I shouted at them and they took off. I chased after them across the square and down a road and with such a huge amount of people I lost sight of them. I staggered breathless back to the others.

When I got back, Natalie was having a tug of war with a child who was hanging on for dear life to a T-shirt. The mother had apparently tried to distract Tom by offering to read his palm free of charge and in the meantime the child had forced the T-shirt off the non-slip hanger and Natalie had caught him. I was furious, having just lost a T-shirt to those boys, and I shouted to the woman and ran over to her and gave her a good kick in her butt with my Doc Marten. She retaliated by swinging her shopping bag, no doubt full of stolen goods, and aimed it at my head. I ducked and then gave her a harder kick on her butt and this time she lost her balance and went down on her knees. She stood up and put a gypsy curse on me! Natalie had retrieved the now stretched t-shirt. They disappeared into the crowd to go and rob someone else.

I realised that this time of the night was ideal for thieves. They knew you were tired and so it was an ideal opportunity for them to strike. We were all so tired and had worked so hard all day, so not fancying having any more altercations with gypsies we packed everything away at midnight. Frede had already gone back to Boulogne, Natalie and Patty went home to Lilliers, Arno slept in the hammock and Tom and I were in the van. It was still noisy but I was so tired I went to sleep and didn't wake up till the morning.

A lot of the sellers had gone by the time I woke up and there was still mountains of rubbish and broken bottles everywhere, but I waded through the mess to the café to do my ablutions. That done we set the stall up again, but it was much quieter than the previous two days so at midday we decided to clear everything away for the last time, as we were exhausted. My black-market bag weighed a ton, and I had no idea how much money we had made. I had not dared attempt to count it in case I got mugged. I was dreading the journey home. Making our way through the rubbish was not easy with so much broken glass, and the last thing I wanted was four flat tires. As we made our way out of Lille I was flabbergasted at the amount of rubbish which was piled up in every road. It looked like a council tip, and I pitied the poor people who would be clearing it up.

By the time I got onto the motorway Tom and Arno were asleep. I was so tired I had the window wide open for the breeze and I had to hold one eye open for fear of falling asleep too.

Back in Boulogne I took Arno home then drove the last few kilometres back to Wierre Effroy. The first thing we did was to count our money. We had taken a massive 20,000 francs! All our problems to set up the new shop were now suddenly a distant memory. Being so deprived of sleep did not hamper my joy. I went to my bedroom and Tom went to his and we slept for hours and hours.

Chapter 9 - Depositing the Money

I woke up as bright as a button the next day feeling like a millionaire. I had the longest bath. I had poured all the money into a lunch box and now it was time to go to the bank and deposit our newfound wealth. Once there I waited patiently in a queue clutching my lunch box full of money. French banks are all open plan and there is no security window between customers and the clerk. When it was my turn I opened the lunch box and started to hand the money handful after handful to the bewildered woman behind the counter. Suddenly she said' No, no, stop' and as fast I was piling it up in front of her she was gathering it up clutching it tightly to her bosom. She said I'd have to go to the Security Room to deposit the money and pointed to a door on the other side of the bank. She helped me stuff all the money back into the lunch box, and told me to press the button on the wall and someone would let me in. I made my way to the security room, having to push past the other customers. French people always stared at me - I knew I didn't dress in the fashion that French women did and there were not many 44-year olds who wore Doc Martens either, but I didn't think I was that odd.

I rang the bell to the security room and the lock was automatically released for me to enter. There was a small lady sitting behind a bullet-proof window, a small compartment to put the money in and a few holes to speak through.

She asked how much money I was depositing. I said I wasn't sure exactly but just over 20,000 francs. She told me I'd have to count it first so I replied that I thought that was her job. I counted it not once but four times and each time I made it something different. I could see she was becoming irritated with me! She suggested I count 1000 franc at a time to give to her. That idea seemed to work and I finally passed her the last handful of centimes - just over 20,000 francs. She was glad to see the back of me.

My next port of call was Monsieur Prudhomme. He was pleased to see me and greeted me with his usual bow. I paid the deposit and rent in advance for the shop. It had barely been in my account for half an hour but at least I had it to pay him. He had such a beaming smile as I handed him the cheque! I noticed he was quite undershot, like a cat called Cassie I had once, so maybe that was the reason for his huge moustache. He was telling me about his weekend he had spent with his parents in Hardelot but his jacket drew my attention, it was worse than the last one he was wearing, a vile yellowish brown with green and orange check. He saw me looking at it. 'Do you like my jacket?' he asked happily. 'Mmmm' I said 'very colourful', hoping he would not guess what I was really thinking. I said I had a lot to do so would have to get on and wished him good day. He shook my hand and, bowing again, he wished me a good day too.

I walked round to rue National and looked through the window of the new shop, then I crossed to the other side of the road to look at it from a distance. It was quite a miserable looking place, so I imagined what it was going to look like after it had been painted and was inspired to call the shop Malice. So the Malice in Wonderland which was so beautifully displayed on the van would serve two purposes, the name of Tom's band and the name of the shop.

The man in Canterbury who sold us the cannabis T-shirts had a friend who was a graffiti artist. I contacted him and asked how much it would cost to decorate the shop, and he quoted £200 plus £80 for the spray paint. That was doable at this moment in time so we made a deal and he told me we would have to paint the inside and the façade navy blue so it would be ready for him to do the graffiti. So it was agreed that he would come to Boulogne four days before we were due to open on the 1st. October.

Next we had to compile a list of things we would need for the shop. First was railings to hang the T-shirts on, and I was permitted to go in the shop and measure the wall space to see what length we needed. We would need a till, and as luck would have it the shop next door sold tills, so I went there and introduced myself as their new neighbour to be. We only wanted a small one and the cheapest was 2,000 francs. By now the mega bucks we earned in Lille were beginning to dwindle and I needed to buy quite a bit of new stock so the till man kindly said I could pay him 600 francs a month. I was happy with that arrangement. Finally we would need coloured spotlights.

As we needed quite a lot of new stock the man from Canterbury said he would give me a month's credit. So everything in theory was arranged, and I was very excited.

We continued to do the markets through September but everyone was back at school and had been spending their money on school accessories instead of T-shirts and smoking accessories.

I collected the keys from Monsieur Prudhomme on the Wednesday while we were at Boulogne market. Monsieur Prudhomme's office was just off Place Dalton. I was really looking forward to opening the Malice Shop. I left Tom at the market and clutching the keys I hurried off full of optimism to rue Nationale and our shop. I unlocked the back door and stood in the middle of the shop looking about me and savouring the moment and imagining what it would look like after the graffiti artist had decorated it.

Tom had organised several of his friends to come and help us paint the shop navy blue, for which we needed several litres of paint, and as the graffiti artist was coming on the Wednesday, we needed the walls and ceiling to be totally dry. I left Tom to oversee the decorating and I went off to do the market. When it had finished I packed everything into the van and drove off to the shop to see how things were developing. I could hear music blasting out of the shop when I turned into rue Nationale, and I was concerned that we would upset the neighbours before we even moved in. The till shop was on one side and a pharmacy on the other, with three old ladies running it, but both shops were closed. I didn't know if they had been driven out by the noise or closed early as it was a Saturday.

I went into the shop and there were seven young men all painting vigorously and all covered in navy blue paint. Music was on top volume and the guys were laughing and shouting to each other so as to be heard over the racket of the music. Someone was putting the railings up; they had worked so hard and I was very grateful to them all.

By early evening they had finished, including the front of the shop, but unfortunately some of the carpet too, despite it being covered in ground sheets.

The graffiti artist arrived on the Wednesday along with the man from Canterbury who had brought the new stock with him. They stayed with us that night and the next day they went off to graffiti the shop. They wouldn't tell us what they were going to do and we were forbidden to go anywhere near.

When it was finished it looked superb; he had sprayed planets, stars, clouds and shooting stars on the façade, and he had written Malice with a flying pack of cards one side and a top hat with ears sticking out of it the other side. Some people thought we were opening a night club, so we put a large sign in the window advertising the grand opening of Malice on the 1st October and there would be a bottle of champagne for the first customer.

The next two days we spent putting up and taking down the railings and they were a real problem, either sagging in the middle or missing their connections by millimetres

Friday we displayed the stock and Tom did the window display. We had bought a tubular mannequin we called James and donned him in a fine t-shirt and jams with a ski cap on his head. The man next door delivered the new till, the telephone was connected and we were ready. Suddenly I remembered I had not taken out any insurance, and the funds had practically dwindled to nothing, so I drove quickly to Marquise to arrange some insurance for the shop. Dear Monsieur Molyeaux wanted 800 francs which was all the money I had left for the grand opening the next day. I asked him if he would accept 600 francs for now and the rest the following week and he agreed.

I was only left with 200 francs and I had to buy a bottle of champagne with that as I had advertised it as a prize to our first customer. We also needed to eat!

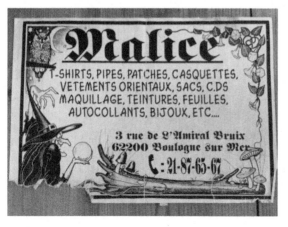

The Malice shop flyer

Chapter 10 - The Grand Opening

Opening day arrived, and Tom had organised an entourage of friends to come and assist us. I had spent the last 200 francs on a bit of food and the cheapest bottle of champagne I could find. Frede and Arno, who had helped us at Lille, arrived soon, followed by Babas who was going to keep the rails tidy and watch out for thieves and Yann who was going to be front of house out on the pavement to do the crowd control. The downside of the day was I had not a centime to put in the till which meant we had no float, but I consoled myself that it was better to have an empty till in the morning than at the end of the day.

The Golden moment arrived; we took our places, Arno opened the doors dead on 10 o'clock and the queue of customers I expected to be waiting were not there, there was no one to be seen.

After a long 10 minutes our first customer came in and it was the annoying boy who repaired kitchen chairs with his father at the market and he would come to our stall and finger all our stuff but never buy anything, we called him 'The Touching Punk'. He bought one post card for 5 francs. 'He's not getting the champagne' I said to Tom, 'Where's my bottle of champagne' he asked, 'sorry, someone was just here before you' I said, so then he was demanding we gave him his 5 francs back, but luckily three more customers came in and we were distracted by them as the touching punk left saying the shop was crap.

The three new customers each bought a t-shirt, and I had to go next door to the pharmacy to change notes, but they didn't mind. When I got back to the shop there were more customers looking at the stuff and admiring the décor and so it continued with a constant flow of people. Yann got slightly over-enthusiastic with his front of house position and gradually turned into an aggressive bouncer frisking people before he would let them enter the shop, I had to go and stop him as he was frightening our customers away.

I made several trips to the pharmacy throughout the day, changing bank notes, and they didn't mind. Later on well-wishers from the market came to visit us - one even brought a bottle of champagne to celebrate.

There was a steady flow of customers. Mid-afternoon a very short man came into the shop wearing a royal blue overall coat reaching nearly to his ankles. He arrived at the counter and introduced himself as Monsieur Petite and promptly placed a large fire extinguisher on the counter. 'No thank you' I said quickly, but he insisted I had to have it, even though I told him it was OK - I had insurance and a bucket of water if we had a fire. I just wanted him to take his fire extinguisher and go, as he was spoiling the so far happy day we were having. He then flapped some papers in my face. I snatched them away from him took one look at them and didn't understand what they said. 'Well OK if it's free I'll have it' I said 'no it costs 1600 francs' he retorted, 'then I don't want it' I said. Arno had joined us and taken over the conversation with Monsieur Petite and told me I was legally obliged to have one in the shop. I looked in the till which was full of money but I didn't want to give him any, so I told him he'd have to come back next week. He demanded a deposit so I offered him 100 francs. He took it and handed me the fire extinguisher and a crash course on how to use it. Thankfully he went, and we continued serving our customers for the rest of the afternoon right up until 7 o'clock. The moment of truth! We totalled the till and we had taken just over 5000 francs, which meant I could pay some of the debts I had accrued during the previous week.

The next day was Sunday and we had the day off to recuperate. It had rained earlier but now it had turned into a warm pleasant evening. I had made a nice dinner and we had the French doors open with a calm breeze coming in. As we sat enjoying our food I heard a rumble and then a cow came charging through the back garden followed by another and another and then a whole herd of cows came stampeding all over the garden running, both sides of the house. I jumped up and closed the door for fear of them coming in, and we rushed to the French doors the other end of the room and there were cows running amok all over the garden and before disappearing down the lane. That's what happens when you don't have a fence at the bottom of your garden, plus they had ruined the entire crop of Farmer Malfois' beetroots.

The next week business was brisk - far better than I ever imagined - so we decided we would stop the markets for the winter and hoped that the shop would make enough money to keep us going. I had found a new supplier in Yorkshire and they had sent a catalogue full of wondrous things. They had pipes of all shapes and sizes even one that was the shape of a credit card, bongs, glass or plastic, little weighing scales, cannabis T-shirts, extra-long cigarette papers, little wooden stash boxes and necklaces with leaf pendants and much more. There couldn't be any harm in selling these things I decided. After all, the tabac shops sold pretty much the same, as in cigarette papers and pipes. My stuff was just not as conventional and besides was in great demand. Tom and I chose the things we liked and I placed a massive order. When it arrived, having got through the customs unopened, Tom made a fantastic display in the glass top cabinet. Our customers were overwhelmed with the choice of smoking accessories at their disposal. We had ordered some cannabis stickers as well so I stuck a few on the Malice van to make it look pretty.

Christmas arrived, and husband said he was coming home for three weeks but actually stayed three days and then went off to a new job in Germany, so he said. I spent New Year's Eve on my own doing a two-sided puzzle, no one rang me at mid-night to wish me a happy new year.

Back at work we had ordered some new T-shirts and this time some waistcoats with cannabis leaves on and 'Legalise Cannabis Campaign' written on the backs. We dressed James the tubular mannequin in one of the waistcoats and a woolly hat with a leaf on the front, he looked fabulous.

We sold quite a few of the waistcoats that week but the following week a young man who had bought the first one came into the shop and told us that he was wearing his new waistcoat and had been stopped by the douanes who had taken him back to their office at the port and confiscated it and asked him where he had bought it. He told them he had bought it from us, but then he said they took his stash which was concealed in the pocket of the waistcoat. I told him he was rather stupid carrying cannabis with him wearing that waistcoat. I really didn't believe that the douanes had the right to confiscate peoples clothing, I suggested he went and asked for it back but he said he was frightened to. I was just worried he'd want his money back.

Friday February 3rd 1995 I paid the last instalment for the till much to the relief of the shop owner next door as it had been a couple of weeks late. We had a good weekend and turned up for work bright and breezy on the Monday morning. I went round to the back door while Tom loitered out the front. As I entered the shop I noticed that the middle glass door was smashed to pieces and there lying in broken bits was the till that I had only just finished paying for three days previous and it hadn't even had any money in it. Nothing had been stolen. I had no idea of who would go to all that trouble just to smash a till, and why didn't the burglary alarm go off? The till went back next door to be repaired and we were back to the lunch box for the duration. My suspicions were aroused when I noticed Lorraine's ex-boyfriend, who she had dumped a couple of weeks previously, loitering on the opposite side of the road staring over at the shop.

I called the police to come and investigate. They did come but just stood there saying there was no evidence of a break-in and started looking at our wares. Then who should walk in but Monsieur Prudhomme; he had seen the police car outside and had wondered what had happened. He said he would come with me to the police station that afternoon to make a statement, which he did.

I met Monsieur Prudhomme outside the police station as we sat waiting to see someone, he kept singing 'Don't Worry, be Happy' over and over again. He was driving me nuts, and when I could stand it no longer, so I asked him to sing something else, and he burst into 'Always Look on the Bright Side of Life'. I was on the verge of doing him an injury, even if it was in the police station. Eventually we were beckoned into a room at the top of a flight of stairs, I gave my statement and I knew that the police wouldn't bother doing anything. It soon became apparent that the intruder had broken in by forcing the electric shutter and breaking it and I had to get it repaired before we closed. Luckily both the till and the shutter were covered by the insurance.

There had been unrest down at Boulogne Port by the French seamen who were protesting against their boss, Stena Line Ferries, who had sacked many of the French seamen and replaced with cheaper Polish ones. There was word that the French seamen were rioting down at the port so what better way to spend an evening than to go and join the rioters.

I went after work and I had never seen anything like it. All the rioters had scarves round their faces or were wearing balaclavas. There were riot police and gendarmes everywhere, no doubt shipped in from other towns, and the big black vans that had brought them there were all parked up in a menacing line to stop the rioters advancing. The vans had metal grills all round them and so did the helmets the riot police were wearing. They also wore gas masks on their faces and carried big shields to protect themselves from the rocks that were being projected at them. I went up to one of the rioters and asked how I could help. He told me to go and collect the broken rocks from the disused railway line, just next to the battle ground and bring them to this point for the rioters to grab and throw at the police. I was pleased to be able to help, so ducking and diving beneath the flying missiles I did as I was asked and joined the many others who had been commandeered to do rock collecting. I gathered as many rocks as I could and went back and put them in a pile. I did this for some time, and no sooner had I deposited one lot than they were gone. There were piles of rocks all over the battle ground.

Then things took a turn for the worse. Suddenly the riot police got into lines, and the front ones held their shields up in front of them while the rows behind lifted their shields above their heads and they stood perfectly still but all the time being bombarded by the rocks hurtling at them. This confrontation continued for some minutes, then the police started to shuffle slowly towards the rioting mob. I was nearly at the front and watched in amazement. Suddenly the police charged at us and sprayed tear gas in our faces. I was the only person without a scarf round my face and I got a face full of gas and I just could not see a thing. My eyes were stinging terribly and all I could do in my blinded state was to grab the nearest person to me and bury my head into his chest where I stayed for a considerable time until my eyesight slowly started to return, though I couldn't open them for long. I never did see who it was I had spent such an intimate time with but with my eyes still tightly closed I thanked him and decided I'd had enough of rioting, so felt my way back to the shop.

The next day was quiet, and at around 11 o'clock a middle aged man came in wearing a track-suit and started looking through the rails of T-shirts, Tom and I grinned at each other because the man was rather old to be looking at the things potentially for young people. He was looking for ages and was concentrating on the tie-dye T-shirts which were on the same rail as the cannabis waistcoats we had started selling recently. Then he picked out a 'Rage Against the Machine' t-shirt and asked if he could try it on. I said he was welcome to, so he took off his track suit jacket and hung it over the rail on top of the tie-dies. He put the t-shirt on and came over to the counter and asked if it suited him, but of course he looked ridiculous in it, it had 'Killing in the Name' written on the back and 'Red Hot Chilli Peppers' on the front, hardly an item of clothing for a middle aged man with a grey crew cut, but I told him he looked wonderful. He took it off at the counter and said he'd take it. I folded it up and put it in a bag, and all the while he appeared to be having difficulty putting his track suit jacket back on, but eventually he did and paid and left.

Later that afternoon I was tidying the T-shirts on the railing found an empty hanger where a cannabis waste coat should have been hanging, I searched for it in the hope it might have been put elsewhere but it hadn't. We concluded that the middle-aged man must have stolen it as there were only a few customers in that day. It also explained why he was having so much difficulty putting his jacket on, as he must have put the waistcoat under his jacket and slipped the two on together. Sadly, we had no proof and because of the nature of the waistcoat it didn't seem a great idea to go and report the theft to the police, so that nasty man had lost us 250 francs.

What puzzled me was why this man would buy a T-shirt for 200 francs and then steal a waste coat with 'Legalise Cannabis Campaign' written on the back of it.

Chapter 11 - Moving On

We resumed the markets in March. Tom kept shop while Arno came with me to Etaples on Tuesdays and Fridays weather permitting. It was in Etaples that I met an English lady called Mary, another stall holder. She lived in Etaples with her French husband Alan who was unemployed at the time. Mary and I became great friends. She was a kind lady and smoked 75 cigarettes a day.

Tom's girlfriend Emelie had a cousin called Eddy and one day she brought him into the shop to meet us, but he was extremely shy and looked very sad. He left it up to Emilie to speak for him. He was very slight and looked not much younger than me, he had long straight brown hair nearly to his waist and he was not much taller than me either. He had big brown doleful eyes with matching dark lines underneath which gave the impression that he hadn't slept for days. He only knew two words in English one was 'shit' and the other was 'bollocks'. Emilie explained that Eddie had not really done anything with his life since he left school, but he had a passion to become a tattooist. She said his artwork was very impressive and he had done a few tattoos on himself and his friends. I told him that he could do his tattoos in the shop if he'd like to and maybe that would start him on the way to fulfilling his dream but I would have to get permission from the shop owner first. Eddie was really happy with my proposition.

Sadly the shop owner did mind and informed me that she had decided to sell the shop and we would have to vacate it by the end of April. I was furious after all that money we had spent on decorating it and we were comfortable there, I didn't believe she was selling it, she just wanted us out. Anyway, we were doing quite well and if Eddie joined us he could help towards the rent so maybe we could find another shop in the town centre. So off I went in search of Monsieur Prudhomme.

I hadn't been able to pay the mortgage since Christmas as husband had not communicated or sent any money for the bills and I didn't know where he was. I paid what I could, but not the Tax Fonciere and Tax d'Habitation, the equivalent of council tax in

England, nor the mortgage. The shop came with electricity and business rates as well as the rent, so things were getting difficult.

Eddie came into the shop one day and said he had seen a shop to let in the town centre on the corner of Rue de la Lampe and Rue de L'Arimal Bruix, the main road which joined Grand Rue that went up to la Haute Ville, the old town, which was surrounded by tall ramparts. The shop had been empty for several months and had previously been a soap shop, Une Savonnerie. It hadn't been very successful and had only lasted for three months. Eddie had made us an appointment to view the shop the next day at 3 o'clock.

In the meantime Monsieur Prudhomme had telephoned to say he had found a prospective shop in Rue de L'Arimal Bruix too, and it had been an employment agency. In fact I seemed to remember going there once when I was looking for a job around the time of the unfortunate newspaper advert.

Eddie came to meet me at the shop, and we set off for our rendezvous outside 'Savilino' and when we got there I did recognise it as the employment agency I had been in. It occurred to me that our next place to visit with Monsieur Prudhomme was this place too. I told Eddie and he didn't answer as the lady was there waiting for us. It was perfect, much bigger than rue Nationale with two smaller rooms off the main shop plus a cellar that also had two smaller rooms. We can have some good parties down here, I thought to myself as the lady babbled on. In the main shop one of the rooms had a glass partition which would be ideal for selling the pipes and bongs and stuff out of view from prying eyes I thought. Realising that Monsieur Prudhomme's rendezvous was imminent I told the lady I had to go and would let her know our decision. So Eddie and I left hastily, leaving the lady to lock the door. We legged it round the block and arrived back at the 'Savilino' only to see the estate agent was still there, so I asked her if she was waiting for more clients to view the shop and she said she was. I had to tell her that there had been a mix up and it was me and Eddie she was waiting for again. She didn't appear to mind and I said I'd contact her soon.

Keen to have the shop but not wanting to look too eager Eddie and I went to the agent a couple of days later to ask her, if we rented the shop would they object to Eddie doing tattoos in there. As soon as we got there the woman said there was someone else interested in it and we needed to make our minds up straight away, but it was just a pressure tactic and I wasn't going to be flummoxed by it. Then we explained that Eddie would be opening a 'Tattooage' in the shop, but she said she would need the proprietor's permission first. So there and then she phoned the man, chatting for a good ten minutes, probably reminding them that the shop had been vacant for 4 months and these clients were better than nothing.

After her phone call she said that it was possible but on the condition that I sublet the room to Monsieur Caffier (Eddie). I agreed and then she asked for three months' rent in advance and agents fees, fourteen thousand francs in all. We didn't have the Lille Braderie to save us this time but I thought if Eddie can contribute we might be able to muster two months' rent and I could say I had misunderstood three months for two, by which time they would have drawn up the contract and wouldn't want the shop without tenants in for another four months.

Eddy borrowed his contribution and I scraped ours together by taking it out of the domestic bill money I had put by at home. The rest was from sales in the shop and markets. So armed with a variety of bank notes and 10-franc coins I set off to the estate agent to sign the contract and pay the deposit. I did not like the woman who was waiting for me and I got the feeling it was mutual. She looked me up and down, but I ignored her stares and just wanted to get on with signing the contract. She was dripping in diamonds, very high heels, and immaculately dressed, sitting with her legs crossed. I was wearing leggings, a t-shirt and Doc Martens. I sat next to her with my legs apart and my toes turned in. She proceeded to read the twenty-page contract which I didn't really understand, but I gave the occasional nod of pretending I did. When she had finished, we both had to initial every page of the contract twice because we each had a copy, after which she gathered up the reams of papers and minced out of the office. Then I had to go to another lady to give her the deposit. I handed her 10,500 francs and waited in anticipation for her to tell me there was not enough money, which she did. She said the agent's fee was missing. No, I assured her, 'there is two months' rent plus your fee 10,500 francs.' 'No Madame' she said 'it is three months' rent in advance'. 'I really thought it was two and I don't have any more' I said. She realised that there was no point in carrying on with the conversation so she agreed, handed me the key, and off I hurried to meet Eddie in the café conveniently right opposite the new shop owned by Belgian born Monsieur Van Pepperstraaten. We went straight away to look at the new shop. Sadly, there was no way I could afford the graffiti artist again so we would have to do our best.

This time we weren't given two weeks to prepare the shop, so everything had to be done over several nights. It was exhausting. Tom, Emilie and Eddie made an attempt to copy the decorations we had in the other shop, all the more difficult as we had to skimp on materials because I had no money. I could only afford to buy white paint and add a colour to mix it. We wanted the background to be dark purple but unfortunately it ended up a wishy-washy mauve. For the planets and stars Emilie made stencils out of lino, and I bought spray cans in white, red and black and although they made a great effort it was nothing like the other shop. Not to worry, we had much more space, plus we were in the town centre.

There was a mad rush the night before the opening of the new shop. After we closed in rue Nationale all the stock had to be packed up and the railings taken down. The two counters were coming with us as I had bought them from the proprietor. All available cars were at the ready and James the mannequin, still clothed, travelled in Arno's 2CV with his top half poking through the sunroof. Thanks to a posse of volunteers we managed to get the shop ready for opening the next day after working well into the night.

I lacked the enthusiasm that I had when we opened the first shop as I was becoming increasingly concerned about our financial situation. We hadn't heard from husband since Christmas or received any mortgage money. I didn't even know where he was, just somewhere in Germany. I had started to receive demands from people I owed money to and it was impossible to pay them on the small income from the shop. I had to make the shop bills my priority but even then, there was hardly any money left to buy food with. It eventually occurred to me that husband had chosen to abandon us.

Chapter 12 - The Incompetent Monsieur Martell

I understood nothing about accountancy, so I had employed an accountant to take on the task of 'doing my books'. The first time I had visited him had been in early January 1994 just after we had done the disastrous Christmas Market at Wimereux and there had been nothing for him to account for as we had only been working for three weeks and he had told me to return to him in a year's time. As I bought my stock in England and paid the VAT over there, I understood that I could then claim it back plus various other expenses by deducting it from the VAT bill I would pay here in France. So on my annual visit to Monsieur Martell the accountant I asked him how I could claim the English VAT back. He could see on the invoices how much I had paid, but he said he didn't know and besides he assured me that I wouldn't have to pay any VAT as I would not be making enough money. I was happy with that so just before we opened the shop I had been back to see Monsieur Martell and suggested I may need a VAT number now as we were going to open a shop. He reiterated that I probably hadn't earned enough money yet and to leave things as there were and he would reassess next time.

In January '95 I had returned with all my invoices, books, papers, till rolls and stock taking lists all mixed up together in a plastic carrier bag, I had never been a tidy person when it came to bits of paper however hard I tried to be. I left it all with Monsieur Martell and he said he would get in touch with me in March which turned out to be the third week in April. When I arrived at his office he was sitting behind his desk with all the tatty bits of paper I had given him previously which now looked like someone had ironed them for they were neatly arranged into months, the invoices, receipts and till rolls. He greeted me by standing up and shaking my hand with his smelly pipe sticking out of the corner of his mouth.

'I've made a terrible mistake' he said. 'OK, well never mind, what kind of a mistake, and did I make a profit'? I asked eagerly. 'A little' Monsieur Marcell acknowledged, '15,000 francs'. Not a fortune but not a loss either. 'That's OK Monsieur Marcell, what is the mistake you made?' I asked. 'I didn't realise how much money your enterprise had taken so in fact you should have been given a VAT number'.

I tried to explain that when I purchased my stock in England I had paid the VAT there, which he could see on the invoices. He then told me that as I had sold the items in France, I had to pay the VAT on them in France. Surely I should be able to claim the VAT back that I had paid in England? He said I possibly could but he didn't know how. So 17.5% VAT in England and 20% in France. The man was deranged! I was really cross with him and asked him how he thought I was going to be able to pay it, but he just shrugged his shoulders and handed me two invoices, one for the 5,000 francs VAT bill and another for 3,000 francs for his services. He knew what he could do with both of them! Before I left, he said I would have to go to the Hotel des Impôts (tax office) and ask for a VAT number. I gathered up the piles of papers on his desk and stuffed them into the carrier bag and left clutching my 'bilan', (balance sheet), while he sucked vigorously on his smelly pipe which had gone out.

We had a daily routine, which was opening the shop and then sitting on the terrace of Monsieur Van Pepperstraaten's café opposite enjoying coffee in the sunshine and waiting for our first customer to arrive. Both well into their sixties, Madame Van Pepperstraaten worked behind the counter making the drinks and the microwaved chips and burgers, while Monsieur Van Pepperstraaten welcomed his customers and in a high pitched voice, half speaking and half singing, and called the orders across the café to his poor over-worked wife.

It was during the first week of opening the new shop, and we were drinking our coffee as usual on Monsieur Van Pepperstraaten's café terrace when three douaniers drove down Rue L'Arimal Bruix and stopped at the junction of Rue de la Lampe. The three uniformed men inside the car were staring at me and Tom for several moments so I stared back and off they went, but I noted the registration number 3307 WK 59 on their white Peugeot 106, which looked very similar to the one that had been outside our house and followed us last June. About 5 minutes later they drove past again still staring. That day I counted 7 times they drove past the shop, and always staring. If we weren't on the café terrace they would wait by the shop door staring in.

The douaniers continued to do their daily drive-pasts, and it became a matter of who could stare the longest. It was during the second week of opening the shop that we had our first spy. I guessed it must have been the guy's first assignment because he had no idea of discretion. He removed each T-shirt one by one off the railing and examined them very closely front and back, especially the T-shirts with anything cannabis related. He looked at every postcard that had a cannabis leaf on it, he did the same with the patches and bandanas. He then moved into the 'hole' where Tom had made a magnificent display of pipes, bongs, pill boxes, and tobacco tins with cannabis designs, extra-long cigarette papers, scales, flags, jewellery and cannabis scented joss sticks.

The spy stood staring at Tom's display for so long I asked him if he smoked cannabis. He didn't answer yes or no but he did ask me if I sold it. I assured him I didn't sell cannabis in the shop so he asked me if I sold it anyway and I told him I didn't. Then he asked me if I smoked it to which I replied that I had done when I was a hippy in the summer of '69, and I added that I was still a hippy. When he had had a good look at everything he said he would come back at the weekend and buy a pipe. But of course he didn't, and we never saw him again.

One Sunday during May there was a braderie being held in Rue Nationale. Frede and Arno had offered to do the early shift there for us as I hadn't felt very much like doing it. I was becoming increasingly worried about the debt I was getting into and still nothing from husband! He must have realised that I would not be able to cover all the bills, and I hadn't paid the mortgage for 5 months now. I took Tom into Boulogne in the afternoon and there were lots of his friends at our stall. I went for a wander round the braderie and then went home for a cup of tea. I wasn't there for long as I had a feeling there was going to be an incident in Boulogne so I went back. When I got there, I was trying to make my way to our stall but everyone seemed to be walking towards me and I had to fight my way through the crowd. I was right, as when I caught sight of the Malice stall I noticed five plain clothes men standing round the tables holding some pipes, T-shirts and stickers. I saw identity cards being checked, then Ann-Sophie, who had been there helping

Tom, spotted me and indicated with her head for me to disappear quickly.

Indeed I am no coward, but I did as I was bid and went into the nearest café. Whilst I was sitting there drinking my espresso, I suddenly remembered that we had received a new assignment of bongs and pipes the day before, and, fearful of the douaniers going to the shop and confiscating them, I hatched a plan. As I still had the key to the old shop, I decided I would go and gather up all the smoking equipment and hide it in the old shop. Just as I left the café en route to carry out my mission I saw Tom and Ann-Sophie being led away on foot surrounded by five men laden with my carrier bags full of my things. I shot back into the café and hid behind the door frame and got some very strange looks from some of the customers. When the coast was clear I hurried along Rue du Bras d 'Or, a back street, which unfortunately meant I had to pass the police station, I didn't know if Tom had been taken there or to the douanes office down at the port and neither did I have time to find out; my aim was to save my bongs.

On arriving at the shop and checking the coast was clear I hastily entered the shop locking the door behind me, and grabbed several carrier bags from behind the counter. I shot into the 'hole' and stuffed all the bongs and pipes and anything else I considered to be at risk into the carrier bags. That done I made a swift retreat back onto the street and made my way to rue Nationale.

Just as I passed the police station and turned the corner who should be coming towards me but Tom and Ann-Sophie also clutching carrier bags.

As we made our way back to the stall Tom explained what had happened. The men were customs officers and they had been taken to the offices at the port. Once there the confiscated items had been laid out on a table and closely examined by the men. Tom and Ann-Sophie had been asked their names, addresses and ages, and as it happened they were both minors so there was nothing to be done. One of the men had made a brief phone call and then another. He appeared to be angry as he slammed the phone down and put the stuff back into the carrier bags and told Tom and Ann-Sophie they could go. I concluded that whatever had been their intent they had been unsuccessful. At the end of the braderie it hadn't been great -

800 francs - but we had managed to hang onto our stuff which had come very close to being confiscated by the customs.

The following week I went to see about a VAT number only to be told I already had one since I started on the market in December 1993. What was wrong with that stupid accountant? As usual, anything I tried to do properly someone always cocked up at my expense. Monsieur Martell could whistle for his 3000 francs and the tax people for theirs.

Chapter 13 - Making New Friends

Since we had been going into Monsieur Van Pepperstraaten's café we had become acquainted with some of the regular customers. One of them was called Michel. I didn't know what his job was, but he worked in an office just up the road from our shop and there were always people looking for him. One day I was sitting on the café's terrace waiting for the douane's daily drive past when Michel joined me and asked if I was having problems with the douanes. I was surprised that he knew and I was even more surprised when he told me that they had been making inquiries at the 'Chambre de Commerce' about the legality of the Malice shop but not the merchandise. They wanted to know if I was registered as a 'commerçant', and whether I had transferred the registration of the market business to the shop. Well, I hadn't because I hadn't known I was meant to. Michel advised me to go and sort it out as soon as possible because the douanes could, if they wished, close the shop down instantly. I asked Michel how he knew that they had been asking questions about the shop. He had a friend who worked there and had told him. He offered to come with me to the Tribunal de Commerce to change the registration. We went there a couple of days later and it cost 1000 francs just to change a piece of paper, which, apart from what it cost, was a relatively simple task which took seconds, and hardly something to jeopardise my business.

A week after I had transferred the registration of the shop I received a phone call from a lady in Lille who was in charge of processing the registration form. She asked me if the shop was a secondary activity to the market, and by this I understood she wanted to know which came first the market or the shop. I explained that I started the market first but since then I had opened a shop, and we worked the markets four or five days a week and the shop was open for six. I didn't mention the Sunday braderies as I didn't want to confuse her. So although the shop came secondary to the market it was the principal activity. I did not know whether I had given her the correct information as I had become quite confused with the complex questions and besides what did it matter? The market was all part of the same business and was just an extension of the shop.

So when I was summoned back to the Tribunal de Commerce and handed yet another stack of paper it transpired I had given the wrong information to the lady in Lille and the all-important tick had been put in the wrong box which meant that the market was the main activity. I repeated what I had told the lady on the phone, she didn't care and said if I wanted to change it I would have to pay 800 francs. I was fed up and wondered if there was some kind of conspiracy going on between the douanes, the Chambre de Commerce and Monsieur Martell the accountant, all trying to bleed me dry. I suppose if they thought I was drug dealing I would have loads of money and be able to pay all these financial errors that they were bombarding me with.

I left the tick where it was and, in any case, whatever tax bills they sent me I couldn't pay them.

Eddie did eventually start his tattooing career in the middle of June 1995. He had borrowed 1500 francs from his uncle to buy the machine and all the accessories he needed. Emilie had made him an appointment book and Eddie had made a catalogue of examples of his drawings to be viewed by potential customers along with business cards which were all arranged beautifully on a table outside his tattooing studio which was next to the toilet, and just as well, as many of his male clients vomited during the tattooing process.

Eddie's first customer was a young lady who had asked for a butterfly to be tattooed on her left breast and Eddie insisted on taking photos of all his work so as to make a portfolio. His business soon got going and he was doing three to four tattoos a day. I was very pleased for him that his dream had finally come true and by the standard of his work he deserved it.

I was getting more and more into debt, and the bills were coming thick and fast and I had been threatened by the huissiers (bailiffs) because I had not paid the mortgage for six months. Tom being a minor was my lifeline, as the law in France is if there is a child in the household then the EDF are not allowed to cut off the electricity and neither are the water company. The bank was not allowed to chuck you out of your house between October and March.

One day I plucked up courage to make a list of all the domestic expenses and shop overheads. There were two phone bills, the shop rent, two rates bills for the house Tax de Habitation and Tax Foncier, plus the rates for the shop charges for being self-employed, of which there were four, obligatory private health insurance, social security, URSSAF (family allowance stoppages), old age stoppages, plus income tax, not forgetting the VAT, and the running costs for the van, three lots of insurance, house, shop and car, plus keeping the shop well stocked so we had an income from it, and then of course we had to eat. And I hadn't included the 6000 francs mortgage. The temptation of becoming a drug dealer was overwhelming but I didn't want to end up in prison so I quickly dismissed that idea. Forever an optimist I chose to live in hope but there was always the chance of me dying in despair.

It was on a lovely hot summer's day that I met Peter Tollmache in the middle of the zebra crossing outside the shop. As we passed each other he raised his panama hat and said 'Good morning to you, lovely weather, what?' We stopped briefly to chat; he spoke so frightfully posh and he looked like someone from a previous decade like the 40's. Unfortunately the rest of Peter was less impressive. He was a tall slim man of about 60 with a brush of grey hair sticking out under his panama hat. He had a kind unshaven face, he wore a cream blazer with stained lapels, his off-white shirt collar was quite frayed and his beige trousers were, to say the least, grubby. He carried a very tatty nylon shopping bag and wore open toe leather sandals. He said he had 'orften' seen me in the market but had never spoken to me. I suggested we move off the zebra crossing and he agreed and offered me a coffee at Monsieur Van Pepperstraaten's café.

While we drank our coffees he told me that he had bought a house in Rue de la Tour Notre Dame and had spent thousands of pounds renovating it and it still wasn't finished and that he had run out of money. He also told me that he had been a free-lance journalist and a spy in Russia in his younger days. I liked Peter and he said he would come to see the shop.

The spies continued to come into the shop on Tuesdays and Thursdays without fail. Always the same old routine - checking the T-shirts front and back, then into the 'hole' to check out the smoking equipment and always asking me if I sold cannabis. So as a precaution and purely for the benefit of the spies we had put up a sign saying that the pipes and bongs were sold solely to serve as ornaments and only people over eighteen could enter the 'hole'.

I had also caught sight recently of various men taking photos of the shop, so that gave me the idea to decorate the window with something pretty to make it worth their while.

So we set about re-decorating the window; we put James the mannequin in the middle wearing a 'Smoke Pot' t-shirt and a woolly hat with a cannabis leaf on the front and a pair of jams. We hung a couple of flags up with cannabis leaves all over them and the girls made strips of paper dollies but instead of dollies they did cannabis leaves which we strung across the top and down each side of the large window, then onto the window we attached posters with pictures of cannabis related things and we added a few green balloons and green streamers to finish it off. It looked fabulous. I was well aware that I was provoking the douanes but if they wanted to be so stupid as to think I was a drug dealer I wanted to ridicule them and give them something to think about, though at the same time I needed to be cautious and not push them too far, so with the help of my French friends we compiled a statement to stick on the window.

ARTICLE L 630 OF THE 31ST. DECEMBER 1970 WITHOUT PREJUDICE. THERE ARE TWO PUNISHMENTS FOR THE POSSESSION AND CONSUMPTION OF CANNABIS. IT IS AT THIS TIME ILLEGAL IN FRANCE AND THE PENALTY IS 500,000 FRANCS OR 5 YEARS IMPRISONMENT OR BOTH. IT IS NOT THE INTENTION OF THE PROPRIETOR OF THIS SHOP TO BE CONSIDERED AS SOMEONE WHO ENCOURAGES PEOPLE TO BREAK THE LAW OR THIS ACT. CONSEQUENTLY I AM NOT INCITING ANY PERSON AS THE LAW STANDS TO BREAK THE LAW.

I stuck it onto the corner of the window. I was pleased with the new look window display and waited to see how long it would be till the stream of photographers arrived.

The Malice shop window display

Chapter 14 - The Pressure's On

We normally had the T-shirts sent over from England by parcel post, but it was quite expensive, so as the Seacat from Boulogne to Folkstone was quicker than the ferry and relatively cheaper I decided to drive to Hastings to collect the order and that way we would have the stuff quicker than waiting for it to arrive by post. I booked myself onto the 10.30 Seacat which would get me to Folkstone at 10.30 local time. I would then have three hours to drive to Hastings, collect the order and be back in Folkstone for the 14.30 return journey to Boulogne and arrive at 16.30. So that's what I did. I was a bit anxious going through the customs in Boulogne as that was where the staring douaniers were located, but the first time I did the journey they just stared and I drove straight through.

The douaniers continued their daily drive-pasts, the spies came into the shop twice a week and the photographers continued to take photos.

The first Sunday in July we were up early to go to Boulogne to the 'Grande Braderie' in the town centre. As the shop was on the corner of the main shopping street we were able to open the shop as well as putting a table outside so we didn't need a parasol on this occasion. On our way to Boulogne, we arrived at the junction where the big round-about was and who should be illegally parked straddling the white chevrons which were bordered by a solid white line where no car might enter under any circumstances, but three of our 'friends', sitting in their Peugeot 106, 3307 WK 59.

I asked Tom to check the wing mirror to see if they were following us but there was quite a bit of traffic behind us and it looked as if they weren't. We continued on and drove through the first set of traffic lights which were green, then, as we were approaching the second set, I realised their car was driving right beside me on my left. Suddenly they turned right in front of me, causing me to do an emergency stop. All three jumped out of their car. One opened Tom's door and told him to get out and at the same time one opened my door and told me to stay in. As Tom was having his pockets searched by a plain-clothes man, the other two were searching through the rubbish in the foot wells. The man my side had his arm between my legs and his head was in my face. I noticed he dyed his hair black! All they found was chocolate wrappers, empty cigarette packets, used tissues and God knows what else. In the meantime the douanier searching Tom's pockets was rewarded with lots of freshly wetted tissues owing to the fact that he suffered with hay fever at its worst first thing in the morning.

During the rummaging I asked them what they were looking for and one replied 'nothing' I asked what the point was of looking for nothing and he said 'for something to do'. Satisfied or disappointed there was no hidden stash on the floor my one then turned his attention to my black market bag I had strapped round my waist and told me to unzip it. I hoped he didn't want to put his hands in whilst it was still attached to my body so I quickly jingled the change inside with my fingers so he could hear. So as quickly as they had arrived they got back in their car and drove off through red lights and into the distance.

We did the braderie and I was half expecting them to turn up again but they didn't and in fact we didn't see them once the following week, but on the Friday I received a letter from the police telling me I had to go to the police station on Monday to see Inspector Wallet in Room 67 at 10.30 a.m; it didn't say what for.

I arrived clutching my letter for my rendezvous with Inspector Wallet. I was asked my name at the reception desk and was told to sit down and be patient. The lobby in which I waited had a drinks machine, a fine display of house plants, music playing and several posters dotted about of wanted men, mostly Moroccans for terrorism.

Presently I was told to ascend the wide curving staircase to the second floor and down a corridor where I would find Room 67 with Inspector Wallet waiting for me. I knocked on the door and let myself in and sat down opposite Inspector Wallet and I bade him a 'good morning' and he bade me one back as he opened a drawer in his desk and produced a folder with my name written on it. He opened it and inside there were several document-type papers. 'What is all this' I asked, and he told me the douanes had sent a complaint about my T-shirts and that I must stop selling them as they were illegal. I told him that was nonsense and they were not illegal. It was clear that they thought they would frighten me but I am fearless and nothing like that was going to frighten me. Inspector Wallet didn't seem to care if they were illegal or not and then asked me what else I sold in the shop, I invited him to accompany me back to the shop and he could see for himself.

I noticed that a group of policemen had gathered at the doorway of Inspector Wallet's office listening to our conversation, so I asked them if they had nothing to do but they just grinned. After that we left and made the short walk back to the shop.

As we arrived at the shop I pushed past Inspector Wallet to warn Tom that I had a policeman with me. He was talking to some customers so I mouthed to Tom that I had a copper with me and he discreetly warned the others.

I showed Inspector Wallet the cannabis T-shirts. The majority of T-shirts were of popular bands. I invited him into the hole to look at the pipes, and he was impressed. He stared into the glass top counter pointing to various pipes and then asked me what one would do with such a pipe. 'What do you think you would do with it?' I asked him. 'Please tell me', he replied. 'You put them on your mantelpiece and admire them of course'. I laughed as I said it. He continued browsing for a time and so I asked him if he liked the things we sold and he said he did. Eventually he thanked me and left.

A week had gone by since my visit to the police station and I hadn't seen one douanier pass the shop, so I decided I would present myself at their office down at the port, but before I went I had Eddy tattoo two cannabis leaves on my legs, one just above my left ankle and the other on my right thigh. I thought they would see them as a point of sale sign.

I would ask them why they had requested me be summoned to the police station to meet Inspector Wallet and why they drove past the shop several times a day. So tattoos done and healed I prepared myself for a visit to the douane's office. I wore a very short pair of tight black shorts and a tight black t-shirt which had British Grass written on the front and the British Gas flame logo on the back, showing off my nice tanned naked legs and my black Doc Martens. So, flaunting my new tattoos, I drove to the port.

With shoulders back, chest out and head high, I marched up to the main door and pushed it. Annoyingly, I should have pulled, and as it rattled and banged it brought the attention of the PAF police (the border police) who had their office on the ground floor, who all came out to see what the commotion was. 'I'm looking for the douanes' I said. 'First floor' I was told. As I was making my way up the staircase I met a douanier who I recognised as one of the three men who had searched the van that day 'Oh it's Madame Malice' he said. I ignored him and walked past him but he had turned round and was following me back up the stairs. On the first floor he led me into a room where there was a man sitting typing. He looked up at me and offered me a seat, then he asked what he could do for me and I told him I would like to know why they had written to the police about my T-shirts. With that five uniformed douanes and a man in plain clothes all filed into the office, so it became quite crowded in there. The man in plain clothes, a nasty little man with a turned up nose and dark beady eyes, took a bunch of keys out of his pocket and proceeded to unlock a metal cupboard which was full of different coloured folders. He picked a yellow folder about 2" thick and placed it on the desk where the man had stopped typing, and, to my amazement, it had my name written in big letters across the front and a long number underneath. 'Is that my life story?' I asked the beady eyed man, laughing. He had now pulled up a chair and was sitting on the end of the desk. He opened the folder and I craned my neck in the hope of getting a glimpse of what was inside, but childishly he lifted up the cover so as to stop me seeing anything. He pulled out a piece of paper and told me it was illegal to sell T-shirts displaying cannabis leaves. 'Who says so?' I asked indignantly. 'The law' he replied.

I asked to see this L630 law that I was supposedly violating and they didn't have a copy of the 'Code Pénal', so I asked how they knew it was illegal if they had no reference to check. He shrugged his shoulders. So, moving, on I asked why they had confiscated the waistcoat which had been purchased by a young man from the shop. The explanation was that the gentleman in question had been wearing it to advertise that he sold cannabis and that they had found 2 grams of it in the pocket of the waistcoat. 'That was hardly big time drug dealing' I said. 'It makes no difference whether it's 2 grams or 2 kilos' he said sternly. 'I've never seen 2 kilos of cannabis' I said, and suddenly all eyes were upon me as if I was lying. Then it occurred to me it must have been one of them who stole the waistcoat from the shop that day last February. So I stood up to give my accusing speech, slightly apprehensive as all the other douanes were gathered round and one of them was blocking the door. He looked Mexican, with a thick black droopy moustache which reached to his chin, and his cap was so far forward on his head he had to tilt his head backwards to see what was going on.

'I know one of you stole a waistcoat from my shop in February' I said. God, the reaction of the man with the folder was terrifying. He slammed his hand down upon the desk making everything on it bounce, his beady eyes darting all over the place, and he shouted at me 'Are you calling us thieves?' 'Yes' I answered. He calmed down and asked me what the thief looked like so I described the man who had been in the shop.

' He was quite old, 45 maybe, grey crew cut, black eyes and a beer gut, he looked something like a Nazi, ugly'. He asked if the man was in his uniform. 'Well, what do you think?'

I suddenly felt I didn't want to be there anymore. I had said my piece, but I did say one more thing to the now calmed man at the desk: 'And one more thing; stop sending spies into the shop to ask if I sell drugs, I don't'. So I left, but the Mexican was still guarding the door. 'Excuse me' I said, and he slowly moved to let me out saying 'See you soon Madame Malice'....

Me on a windy day on the Seacat going to buy stock in the UK

Chapter 15 - Forewarned is Forearmed

The van did not have its original engine but instead a super diesel engine capable of great speed not in keeping with the rest of the van. I had had a trip to Hastings to buy stock and in a rush to get back to Folkstone, I was bombing along the M20 at 150 kilometres per hour and the van was rattling and banging with the vibration. I didn't want to miss the Seacat. Then in my wing mirror I noticed that both the back lights had fallen out of their sockets and were hanging down the sides of the van, so if I indicated the cars behind me didn't know my manoeuvre. Only I could see the light flashing, not a great situation to find myself in, but I continued at great speed.

I arrived at Folkstone just in time to follow the last car onto the parking deck on the Seacat, but before I went up into the lounge I tried to stick the lights back into their sockets. One of the crew members saw what I was doing and offered to do it for me. I was very grateful and left him to it.

Alighting the other side with side lights back in their sockets I was stopped by the douanes. They did the usual rummage and removed the boxes of T-shirts and other things I had bought, and I was told to follow them into the building and up the stairs I was tired and not in the mood for all these questions they were going to ask me. There were three of them today, and they pulled everything out of the boxes looking at all the cannabis stuff. I had bought some postcards with cannabis leaves on and they seemed particularly interested in those. They asked the same old things and told me the stuff was illegal and I argued that it wasn't, then to change the subject I suddenly asked one of them why French women didn't shave their arm-pits. One of them answered that some did and then carried on with the interrogation. Eventually Lorraine turned up and asked me for the key to the shop as it was gone 7 and they wanted to close, and with that I was allowed to go, along with my stuff. I'm sure that those douanes just wanted to chat for something to do.

Rockstock 2 was approaching and we had to start getting the live music organised, so we put an announcement in the window of the shop asking any bands who would be interested in playing there to come in with their demo tapes. In the meantime I had to try and persuade Phillipe the farmer to allow us to use one of his fields for the occasion. He hummed and ha'ed, saying it depended on the weather because he would have to cut the grass beforehand, and if the weather had been very dry then the grass would not have grown long enough to cut so we would not be able to hold Rockstock 2 there, but on the other hand if there had been sufficient rainfall the grass could be cut in the middle of August and we could use his field. I really needed something more definite than having to rely on an amount of rainfall, as I needed to start advertising. I decided that we had a few weeks yet to start worrying about the length of Phillipe's grass.

For peace of mind I decided I would take some of the problem items in the shop to an avocat to find out for certain if the cannabis T-shirts, pipes, bongs and everything else with a cannabis design on was or was not legal. If he was going to tell me they were illegal then I would have to consider stopping selling them, in theory! I didn't really fancy going to prison for five years for inciting the use of cannabis, although I hadn't physically forced anyone to smoke it and besides 95% of my customers already did and the other 5% wanted to but couldn't afford it.

Appointment made with Monsieur Charpentier, he had told me to bring one of each item, so I arrived at his office in La Vielle Ville (the Old Town) with two carrier bags full of my illegal, or maybe not, merchandise. He was very handsome and tall and well-built with lots of dark curly hair. He welcomed me into his office and asked me to sit down. He cleared a space on his desk and as I placed the objects in front of him he had a big grin on his lovely face and one by one he examined each item more closely. He had a big heavy book open on his desk and as he picked up the bong he started to read aloud but too quickly for me to understand what he was saying. After a moment he said smiling 'these things are not illegal Madame Pattinson' and as he picked up the bong I noticed he handled it in such a way it was probably not the first time he had come into contact with one, and he said 'you have the right to sell this water pipe' and I could see by the twinkle in his eye that he knew very well the purpose of the bong. Then as I put everything back into the carrier bags he said 'I might like to buy this and maybe put a rose in it or just use it for an ornament' as he placed it carefully on his desk.

I thought I was going to get a sale in the avocat's office. There was a t-shirt with a Rasta man lying on the grass with a joint sticking out of his mouth and the logo was 'Don't Cut the Grass Smoke it'. Monsieur Charpentier warned that the t-shirt and the patch like the one I had on my kepi which said 'Smoke Pot', with a cannabis leaf on it, might be seen as inciting people to smoke cannabis, but all the other stuff was fine.

I told Monsieur Charpentier how the douanes had been harassing me and sent spies into the shop, and twice we had been stopped in the van and about the people taking photos of the shop. He said they were trying to frighten me, and as for the visit to the police station, he would write to the Procureur de la République to ask exactly what the reason for the douane's complaint against me was.

With that I paid Monsieur Charpentier 200 francs and left, and it was the best 200 francs I had ever spent. So now I was fully armed against those douanes and police, the next time they would dare to stop me I would be ready for them.

On my next trip in the Seacat I was a foot passenger. I had arranged to meet Brian, the T-shirt supplier, in Folkestone, to collect the Rockstock T-shirts. The Seacat for once was running on time and I arrived back in Boulogne carrying a heavy box of T-shirts we had had made just for Rockstock 2 with the logo and dates on the front and a list of the bands on the back. The long walk from the Seacat to Passport Control was far too long, first you had to wind your way down a never ending zig-zag walk-way, then along the side of the railway track, then you were obliged to cross the railway line, down through a tunnel and up a steep flight of steps through a large hall, and eventually arrive at the passport control knackered. The box had become so heavy I quite enjoyed the wait in the queue, as I could kick the box along the ground. Finally my turn came, and the PAF asked me what I had in the box I said '50 Rockstock T-shirts and two kilos of cannabis' he glanced at my passport and said 'thank you'. He either hadn't heard what I had said or he didn't care but it had amused the man standing behind me.

Phillipe had graced us with the use of his field for which I was very grateful, and the immediate neighbours had, like the previous year, gone away for the weekend. So the Friday was a busy day. I left Lorraine on her own in the shop and she was busy all day selling

Rockstock 2 tickets. Tom and several of his friends were in the field helping with Fi-Fi's scaffolding from Pont Brique to make the stage, the EDF were connecting a large cable to the lamp post which was going to supply us with electricity. I dumped the T-shirts in the shop and went straight out to find some red and white rolls of tape to cordon off the field to stop people jumping over the ditch and getting in for free. Driving around Boulogne I noticed a group of EDF men working on the road. I stopped and asked them where I could get some tape and they directed me to a shop opposite the Liane River. I bought two reels and drove home to give to someone to do the cordoning off, then back to the shop to collect Lorraine.

Saturday morning, Rockstock day, Lorraine was back in the shop but Eddie was there today doing a tattoo on one of his clients. Tom was in Phillipe's field waiting for the man to arrive from Marquise with the P.A. sound system and the bands, which were playing that afternoon and evening, to do their sound checks.

I went out with last year's stolen panels to put them from all directions on the outskirts of Boulogne and Wierre Effroy, hopefully leading the masses to Le Trou D'Enfer. Rockstock 2 was due to begin at 4 o'clock and people who were camping could arrive from 2 o'clock. One field was designated as a car park with directional arrows outside, and the camping would be in the same field as the concert. We had sold masses of tickets but I was thinking some people might try and sneak in for nothing, so I had a rubber stamp made with Rockstock 2 on it to stamp people's hands who had tickets and so hopefully would catch out those who didn't. At 1 o'clock I went back to the shop so Lorraine and Emilie could go home as they were in charge of the entrance, and at 4 o'clock I closed, as I expected that any customers we might have had would be heading for Wierre Effroy. I was in a hurry to get home to see if anyone had turned up yet. En route I passed several young people trekking along the auto-route and along the lanes carrying tents and ruck sacks.

The front and back of the Rockstock T-shirts

When I got home Phillipe's field was full of little tents. Lorraine informed me that the first band was still doing its sound check and there were still four more bands to go. Apart from the sound check delay everything else was going according to plan. Two men were organising the parking, the beer had arrived and a nice stall had been set up for that. I had invited a 'friterie' to come and sell food. He arrived in good time and parked his van in the middle of the field. The stage was up in the far corner, equipped with lighting and a sound system.

There were lots of people, and many had come from as far away as Paris, Arras, St. Omer and Le Touquet. I had heard that Rockstock 2 had been advertised on various local Radio Stations by friends of some of the bands.

So far the weather had been sunny but there were clouds forming on the horizon and rain had been forecast. If it did rain there might be problems, as there was no cover on the stage and there were miles of cables and multi-socket extensions everywhere.

The field was packed with young people and four hours behind schedule the first group started to play. The crowd moved towards the stage and soon got into the mood. I went to help Lorraine at the entrance gate but it was getting dark and soon we wouldn't be able to see anything. A friend had a contraption which was two car head lights attached to either end of a long pole and the idea was to connect to the car battery, but there was no room to put the car, so the battery was removed from the car and brought over to the entrance. When the time came to illuminate our spot the friend came to attach the lights to the battery, we waited in anticipation then the moment of truth and 'voila' there was light but no brighter than that of a car cigarette lighter; we still couldn't see a thing. I went to see Phillipe to ask him if he could do anything and within moments he came rumbling towards us across the next field in his tractor like a super hero with headlights blazing. The only downside of that was he had to leave the engine running which was rather noisy.

All the bands did their stints and in the thick of it all was one of our customers called Punky who was very drunk and wanted to get involved with the group Black Dust, a heavy metal band who were playing. The type of music they played had an effect on people by getting them worked up into a mad frenzy, so they were getting up on the stage and diving into the crowd in the hope that they would be caught by others in front of the stage. Punky in his drunken stupor clambered up onto the stage and chucked himself off it but nobody caught him and he fell to the ground with a thud. Yelling in agony I was obliged to go home and ring for an ambulance which turned up and took him off to Boulogne Hospital with his broken ankle.

The final band was the very popular Liebemachnr, a punk band from Boulogne. They played one song and it started to rain, and after twenty minutes it was bucketing down but they carried on and the crowd were loving it. I was worried they'd all be electrocuted but they weren't. Everyone watched the concert till the end, although we all froze nearly to death watching them. When it was all over I went home, leaving the soggy crowd to get into their soggy tents, and I snuggled up in my comfortable bed.

Major problem the next day: the friterie hadn't shown up and everyone was starving.., I had told him to come back in the morning and by 2 o'clock there was still no sign of him and then I noticed that many of the concert goers through starvation had begun to eat Phillipe's maize and were flattening his neat rows of cultivated crops which he grew to feed his livestock through the winter and was not meant for human consumption. The evidence was clear and I hoped Phillipe wouldn't mind.

Nevertheless the concert recommenced at midday. The weather had become cold and windy and by early evening the crowd started to disperse at the same time as the friterie decided to show up. I asked him where he had been and he thought he was meant to return in the evening. So as soon as he had set up there was a stampede of starving customers.

Rockstock 2 had been very successful and more than 800 people had turned up. It had been exhausting and now I had the next day to clear up Phillipe's field with a host of volunteers and one week to organise our second trip to the Lille Braderie.

Chapter 16 - More Harassment

I was under pressure getting everything ready for Lille Braderie. Emilie and Michelle were going to look after the shop and on the Wednesday I had planned to go to England and buy as much stock as I could from the Hastings supplier. The bootleg man from Canterbury had agreed to let me have everything from him on 'Sale or Return'. I had also made a huge order for pipes and stickers and all that sort of thing. We were going to meet Natalie and her boyfriend Christophe in Lille and Frede and Arno were going to meet us there to help.

The van was showing signs of old age and was slowly falling apart. One of the hinges on the back door had rusted away and broken and my door wouldn't close properly so when I was driving I had a constant cold breeze blowing on my left hand and the body work had started to corrode.

I did my trip to Hastings and bought as much stuff as possible, and driving back as fast as I could on the M20 the side lights fell out of their sockets again. When I got to Folkstone the bootleg man was waiting for me and when I went to put the box of T-shirts in the back of the van I noticed that the door lock cylinder was no longer in the back door, which meant that we could never lock it again. On the Seacat a crew member stuck the back lights back in their sockets for me. I arrived in Boulogne and drove through passport control without any problems.

We did well again in Lille, although there were fewer people, and we caught the odd thief and missed a few too. We had frequent visits from three CRS men who kept telling me to stop selling the cannabis T-shirts, so I put them back in the van and took them out again when they had gone. We decided to go home on the Sunday, but with the takings I was able to pay some domestic bills which was a relief.

Back in Boulogne we still had the daily drive-pasts from the douanes staring in the shop or if we were at Monsieur Van Pepperstraaten's café they would be staring at us. Peter Tollmache popped in occasionally or joined us in the café for a coffee. One day he was going to England to visit his sister Susan in Bexhill and he was getting the Seacat as a foot passenger, and as it was a nice day I

walked with him to the port chatting about this and that. He was
carrying a suitcase so I presumed he would be there for a few days. I
walked with him till he got to passport control and I said goodbye.
As I walked away I turned round to see if he had gone in and I
noticed he was being questioned by three douaniers. I watched for a
moment and then they took him off into the office building. Oh dear,
I guessed they thought he was involved in the drug smuggling I
didn't do. Poor Peter! I hoped he wouldn't miss his crossing.

The next day there was Peter at the shop doorway and he said he
had been questioned by the douanes and they had asked him if he
knew me, how long had he known me, how well did he know me,
then they asked him to open his suitcase, he did and to the douanes
disappointment it was full of apples that had come from Peter's apple
tree in his garden and he was taking them to his sister Susan. I
laughed so much. How stupid they must have felt, how could they
think that dear old Peter would be smuggling drugs. The next time
they drove past the shop I pointed at them and laughed and they
looked away that time.

I had noticed recently that a policeman on a motor bike had been
following me when I'd been driving round Boulogne. He wore
leather boots up to his knees, a leather coat and a German steel
helmet which looked like a relic from WW2. He looked like the
Gestapo. One day he did pass by me waving his hand for me to pull
in, so I did. He got off his motor bike and removed his helmet and
marched up to my van. I opened the window, he was scary, he had a
long thin face and a nasty thin moustache. I smiled at him and
politely said hello. He asked to see my driving licence which I found
in the glove compartment and handed to him. It was my English
licence which he examined closely. He told me it was illegal and that
I would have to get a French one. I told him not to be ridiculous,
mine was enough proof that I knew how to drive whatever language
it was written in and having a French licence would make no
difference to my driving ability. He didn't care what I had to say and
said he would give me one month to change it and then I must
present myself at the police station with my new French driving
licence. I couldn't do it because as far as I was concerned it was an
unnecessary expense and I had far more important bills to pay.

Reminders were arriving every day, and the mortgage worried me more than anything else as I hadn't paid it for nine months, and now I had threatening letters from a Huissier de Justice (bailiffs).

I had been to the EDF office and explained that husband had abandoned us and although I worked I didn't have very much money. They were quite sympathetic and told me to pay something every month. I went to the Bureau des Impôts (rates office) and told them the same sob story but they weren't so sympathetic. The phone at home was going to be cut off at any moment but it didn't matter as we had one in the shop.

If the bailiffs were going to come I needed to hide my pride and joy, my piano, so I asked Phillipe if he could hide it in one of his barns. He said he would but getting it down his long drive-way was another story, not to mention down our drive which was steep and just had loose stones on it. We needed several strong men as the piano was made of solid teak and weighed a ton. Husband had a contraption in the garage which he would lie on when he was working under his car. It was basically a wide piece of wood with wheels on it and that would have to do. We got a posse of Tom's friends to help move my beloved piano down to Phillipe's barn. I couldn't bear to look when it was being moved and the house felt empty without it and there was only a pile of dust that had accumulated behind where it had stood. I was sad and fed up with the financial state of affairs husband had inflicted upon us, but that was too bad, when the piano had reached its destination in the cold draughty barn I went and covered it up with lots of blankets, and we left it on the wheels.

The next time I went to England to buy some stock I was stopped on my way out by the douanes and I hadn't anything in the van apart from the usual chocolate wrappers, empty cigarette packets, dirty tissues and my kepi. I was told to get out and stand by the wall, and one of them arrived with something that looked like a hoover. They opened the back doors of the van where my kepi was and he picked it up and started hoovering the inside of it. I just laughed and asked him why on earth was he hoovering my kepi? He said they would test the contents of the hoover after to see if there were any traces of drugs. I wouldn't say that there had never been the odd joint smoked in the van but even if their hoover got the minutest grain it wasn't going to prove I was drug dealing. After they had hoovered my kepi they then hoovered the van front and back. I missed my crossing because of them but had a nice clean vehicle for which I thanked them. I never heard anything about their car cleaning day.

As Christmas approached I had an idea; we bought a smallish Christmas tree in a pot with roots and some string, tied the branches together to make seven leaves the longest in the middle and going down in size either side till it looked like a cannabis leaf and instead of adorning it with baubles we made pretend joints and hung on it and stood it proudly on the step outside the shop door. It would give the photographers something different to take and the douanes something different to stare at. I don't know what the douanes thought of our Christmas decoration but they never told me to remove it nor did they try to take it away.

Christmas came and went for us and we were in a new year and I hoped our financial situation wouldn't get any worse. The bailiffs had not yet arrived to remove our goods and chattels and we still had electricity. Sometimes when we got home there would be a pile of logs outside the front door that Phillipe had left there for us to put in the log burner. In the garage there were a few lumps of sleeper that husband used to crank his car up with when he was working on it, so when we had nothing to burn I would stick one of his sleepers on the fire but they were quite big so half the sleeper was in the fire and the other half out and we had to push it in as it burned. They also stank of tar, but kept us warm.

After my experience with the douanes and their hoover I decided I would have a game with them, so I rolled a couple of joints minus the cannabis and hid them where I knew the douanes would look the next time they searched the van. I put one large Golden Virginia roll-up in the glove compartment and the other in the side of my door.

The Malice Christmas tree

It was January and I had to go to England to buy some T-shirts, but
not many as we were very short of money. One good thing was that
the Channel Tunnel were offering a day return for 90 francs, so I
went via the Shuttle. It was a cold day and the draft coming through
my broken door kept my left hand frozen. I got to Hastings, bought a
few T-shirts and some post cards and returned to Cheriton with the
back lights hanging out of their sockets by the time I arrived there.
Going through the French border control they took my passport and
told me to park my van in some kind of garage. I was questioned
where I had been, where I was going and all the usual stuff. I was
told to get out of the van and two women arrived and took me off to
an office. These women were to say the least hideous. One had a
moustache and a fat face with fat cheeks, fat lips and pale green
eyes, the other had short back and sides and a spiteful face. I was
told to sit and then nothing happened. I guess they were waiting to
see if they found anything in the van. After a good half hour two
female customs officers walked into the office, one carrying a
selection of the cannabis T-shirts and post cards, the other wearing a
pair of examination gloves and holding as far away from her body as

possible my two pretend joints. She looked at me in such a way thinking 'ha we've got you now'. I so wanted to laugh and say to her 'oh no you haven't', but I didn't in case I aggravated the situation.

Now two customs men had come into the office. I always seemed to gather a crowd when I had any dealings with these people. The woman carrying the joints asked the other one to put some paper on the table, then she carefully put them down and proceeded to dissect one of the joints with great precision opening it up with a razor knife and slowly bit by bit rolling the tobacco thoroughly through her fingers whilst the others looked on in readiness to arrest me when she found the illegal substance. Nothing detected in either, it had taken a good hour before they were satisfied that my joints were nothing else but rolling tobacco. I thought I would be on my way, but no, I was accompanied by the two ugly women to a concrete cell that had a thin strip of wood sticking out of the wall supposedly to sit on. I was then told to remove my clothes. I said it was too cold in there but I had no choice. One woman was standing by me and the other was perched on the edge of the seat. I removed my Doc Martens first which the woman looked at and stuck her hand in checking there was nothing in them, then every piece of clothing I removed the woman sitting down took it from me, looked at it and placed it on her far side where I couldn't reach it. When I had undressed to my bra and pants I hoped I could stop. I was freezing, but they told me to take everything off. I asked if I could put my Doc Martens back on as my feet were cold, so she handed them back to me after I had removed my pants and bra. For a brief moment I thought at 8 stone I had a much nicer body than those two horrors that were staring at me, so there I was stark naked wearing nothing but my unlaced Doc Martens. Then I was told to put my arms out to shoulder level and open my legs, having done that the woman then stuck her head between my legs and told me to cough, I coughed, then she told me to cough again. By now I was so cold I was shivering and my teeth were chattering but I asked her what the hell was she expecting to happen down there. She didn't answer but, satisfied I wasn't concealing a kilo of cannabis on my person they gave me back my clothes. I tried to dress myself quickly but I was too cold to do it in a hurry. Finally we left the cell and I hoped I could go. But no, still not; I was then taken outside by a customs man to a large building on the opposite side. I had no idea where my car was, and they hadn't returned my T-shirts and post cards.

So the next place must have been the Tunnel HQ. I was taken into a large room and told to sit down on a chair. It was busy with people all sitting in front of computer screens. He spoke to a man in plain clothes who eventually came over and asked me more stupid questions and then he went back to his computer. I had been there for two hours and I wanted to go home. I was bored and hungry and wanted a hot drink. After some time I realised the chair I was sitting on had wheels, so I started to push myself towards the other side of the room backwards and nobody noticed. I parked myself in front of a computer screen but before I had a chance to look I was told to turn round and stop looking at it which I did for a few moments and then I turned the chair round again and took a further look at the screen. The man was getting cross and told me to stop. I was clearly getting on his nerves. I sat quietly for a bit longer then I decided I'd venture further into the nerve centre of the Channel Tunnel and rolled myself backwards again to the opposite side of the room, but the man who had spoken to me earlier spotted me and told me to stop. After a few minutes I saw a man who was not in front of a computer screen so with one huge push with my feet I aimed myself at this man and to his surprise I stopped right beside him and demanded a drink. The other man got up from his desk, grabbed the back of my chair and pulled it away from all the activity that was going on and left me sitting in a corner. I told him I wanted a drink, please. I said I'm going to die if I don't have one, and it worked and he went off and came back with a coffee.

I sat quietly and as the people in the office started to go home the man came over and told me I couldn't return to France. 'My children are there and I have a house in Wierre Effroy, I've got to go home' I said. Again he said I couldn't, and I told him my children where minors so I couldn't abandon them. Off he went again for ages and when he came back, he said I could return to France but I would have to be accompanied by an officer.

This was ridiculous. I hadn't done anything wrong. What the hell was the matter with these people? Seven hours after I arrived at the Channel Tunnel I was going home accompanied by this man who was really just hitching a ride back to France, and they hadn't given me my stuff back nor the tobacco from my roll-ups. There was my van still in the garage with the back lights still hanging out. I put them back in their sockets in front of my passenger. I don't know what he thought of his mode of transport that evening but I bet he had never been a passenger in such a dilapidated old banger. When we arrived in Sangatte he went his own way and I went mine.

I got home at midnight and Tom not knowing what had happened had gone home with Arno.

Chapter 17 - The Marriage Spent

After the indignities with the French customs in Cheriton I commandeered Eddie to tattoo a stoned douanier on my left buttock so the next time I was stripped naked it would give them something to look at, and with a few puffs of calming substance I committed myself to Eddie's needle.

I had not paid the mortgage for one year and we hadn't been thrown out of the house. I had stopped opening the letter box at the end of the driveway as the only letters I received were demands for money and the bills were piling up and I didn't want to see any of it, but we carried on regardless in the hope that something would happen and it did - I just got deeper and deeper into debt.

The shop was quiet this time of year, but I had to keep up with the rent and the other bills, and the douanes continued to do their daily drive-past, staring in at us, and things had become very miserable.

For a bit of entertainment I got Eddie to draw the 'finger-up' sign and I took it to the newly opened photo copiers in Rue Faidherbe where it was possible to have it printed onto paper that had a sticky side so you could pull the back off and stick your 16 stickers where you pleased. That evening I went to the port and saw the douanes' cars all lined up parked in their spaces. I parked my van at the other end of the car park and with stickers in hand made my way across the large car park to the douanes' cars. I snuck between the bonnets and the wall and stuck a finger-up sticker in the middle of each of the car bonnets, then I crept round to the back and did the same on the boots. All of a sudden I heard the door to their offices rattle and a douanier was shouting at me asking what I was doing. I upped and ran as fast as I could and sensed that I was being chased. I arrived at my van and looked back where there were two douanes puffing and panting across the car park trying to catch up with me. I thought it would be rude to just drive off after all their running, so I stood tapping my fingers on the roof of the van till they caught up. Poor old fellas! They escorted me back to their cars and asked why I had done it and I said as a present for them, and they made me pull them all off and warned me if I did it again I would be in trouble.

The Gestapo caught up with me eventually and asked to see my driving licence, which was still a UK version, so he threatened me with a fine and gave me two more weeks to get a French licence. The only way I could temporarily resolve the issue was to de-face my English one, so at the top of my licence where it said Counterpart Driving Licence I wrote in bold underneath 'OK to drive in France' and hoped this would be a temporary distraction to the Gestapo.

Shortly after that incident I was followed and stopped by two gendarmes on motorbikes who asked to see my driving licence. I handed it to one of them and he straight away saw the graffiti on it and questioned me, asking if I had written it on there myself. I said I hadn't and that's how English licences were issued, and he confiscated it and said I would have to go to their office to get it back the next day. I decided that the two gendarmes could have done me a favour and if the Gestapo should stop me again I would not be able to show it to him so I didn't go to the gendarme's office to collect it.

We struggled on and I started back at the markets in February but they were quiet too and the police would turn up and tell me I couldn't sell my T-shirts so I would put them back in the van and then out they would come when the police had moved on.

Lorraine came home for Easter and had become quite friendly with the guitarist from the punk band Liebemachnr and was spending a lot of time with him whilst she was home, but her holiday soon came to an end and she was back at university and I had deposited her at Boulogne port to take the Seacat to Dover.

As I was driving out of the port the chief douanier jumped out of a door and stopped me. He asked me what I was doing there and I explained that I had brought my daughter to take the Seacat to Dover, then to my amazement he asked me who I was. 'What sort of a question is that'? I asked him, 'you know who I am'. He replied that he knew me as Madame Pattinson but he wanted to know who I really was. Then he stuck his face right in my face and said, 'why are your eyes funny?' 'maybe because I haven't been up long' I replied, wondering what on earth he was implying. 'No' he said 'you have taken something, what have you taken?' 'I had a cup of tea at home this morning' I told him. He insisted I had taken something and he said he had a machine that could prove it. 'Go on then' I challenged him. Then he asked me all kinds of questions, where was I born, where I lived in England, what my job history was and again who I was. When I insisted I was me he told me to go home and get my birth certificate and all my papers concerning the move to France, and to return there before midday. He never produced his drug detecting machine so I went home and got him all the stuff he had asked for.

Back at the port I took my papers into the douanes' office and put them on their desk. They were gathered up and no doubt photocopied in duplicate, returned, and I left.

I was getting fed up with all this harassment and had a great desire to tell these stupid idiots where to go but if I did that I would most likely end up in trouble so I thought it a good idea at the time to get Eddie to tattoo on my left wrist the 'finger' so when they stopped me I only need to expose the tattoo and it would say it for me. Eddie was not keen to do that tattoo and kept asking me if I was really sure I wanted it done but at that time I did.

The next time I was stopped by the Gestapo I told him I didn't have my driving licence anymore. He said I would have to follow him back to the police station so I drove behind him. When we arrived there he took me into a room where there was another man in uniform and in front of this man he started shouting at me. I suddenly became extremely cross; how dare he shout at me like that - so I removed my black market bag which was full of change from around my waist, raised my arm and with all my might I whacked him with a powerful blow to his shoulder, then fearful of the consequences of my wrath I was relieved when he burst out laughing, and thought my violent action towards him was funny and so did his colleague. I was so cross I was shouting back at the Gestapo telling him that husband had abandoned us and I did not have money to waste on stupid things like a driving licence which would just say the same as my English one. Well that's what I wanted to say but when you are angry and shouting in a foreign language it's not easy to concentrate on what you're actually saying. When I had finished the Gestapo told me I should go home and come back when I was feeling less aggressive. I was embarrassed but I promised him that I would look for my licence and change it. That's what I said, but I had no intention of doing so.

I met Michel, the nice man in Monsieur Van Pepperstraaten's café, one day and when I told him about the desperate financial situation I was in due to husband abandoning us more than a year ago, he suggested I should make an appointment with the British Consulate Monsieur Gérard Barron, whose office was in Boulogne Haute-Ville Rue Saint Jean, so I made an appointment to see him.

Monsieur Barron, bilingual, was a very nice quiet man and made me feel welcome. I sat down and started to tell him of the terrible financial situation I was in and that it was not my fault and had come about because husband had abandoned us. He was sympathetic and listened to me. He was the first person to understand the hopeless situation I was in. I ultimately started to cry as it became evident to me that I could no longer cope alone.

When I had finished telling him my woes and regained my composure he first of all suggested I start divorce proceedings, but as husband's whereabouts was unaccountable he would contact the police to put out a search warrant for him. Then he told me to go home and pack some stuff and go back to England. I told him I had never run away from anything and I wasn't going to now. I would face adversity with fortitude and I would get through this somehow and besides I couldn't just pack up and go back to England as I had two cats and a dog and they would have to go into quarantine and besides that we had the house and my son was settled here and more so I didn't want to go back to England and couldn't have afforded the fare for one foot passenger for one thing let alone a van. He said in that case the next best thing was to sell the house.

So with divorce proceedings in hand and a warrant to look for husband who was as far as I knew in Germany which was not under French jurisdiction and the decision to sell the house I came out feeling a bit more positive than when I went in.

Business did start to pick up and I managed to save enough money to go to England to buy a bit of stock and Tom came with me. Emilie and Michelle kept shop. When we got to Hastings I popped in to see my friend who had put the new brake pads on the van when we had come to England with the 14 fans, and he said he had a present for me and went to fetch it. When he returned it was an 'unused' blow-up doll. Why would I need one of those? But I guessed we could stick a T-shirt on it and use it as a model, but I wished it didn't have its mouth wide open!

With T-shirts and other things for the shop purchased we headed back to Dover, as usual the back lights fell out of their sockets on the M20 and the kind crew members repaired it during the crossing. I had said to the guys that there was a blow-up doll in the back of the van if they wanted to play with it..

Arriving in Boulogne we went down to get into our vehicles and there was the blow-up doll stuck to the back window. I did not have time to remove it so we had to drive through customs with it gawking out at them. Just as we drove past one of the douaniers bashed on the roof of the van and ordered me to stop, as he came to the window I could see he was laughing but trying to cover his face so I wouldn't see. He told me that ' poupée gonflable' blow-up dolls were 'interdit' forbidden in France and told me to get out of the van. Up the stairs to the now familiar office I was told to sit and as one douanier placed himself in the doorway the other two got the ever growing folder out of the cupboard. Did I know that 'poupées gonflables' were illegal in France? 'I'm sure they are not' was my defence. 'In fact' I lied 'the one in my van was made in France'. They asked me what I was intending to do with it and I said it was Tom's and regretted saying it as soon as I had. Poor Tom, sitting patiently in the van, was being blamed for something nothing to do with him. I was hoping they would strip search me so I could show them my tattoo of a stoned douanier but sadly they didn't and I was allowed on my way. They hadn't even checked the T-shirts I had brought back with me. Tom had given up waiting and had walked back to the shop.

Chapter 18 - The Raid

It was 18 months since husband had abandoned us and I had reached the lowest point in my life, that awful feeling which came over me every morning when I awoke remembering the dreadful financial state of affairs I was in, then anxiety spreading over my body like ink on blotting paper. I had no one to talk to, no one to put their arms round me to reassure me that things would get better and no one who cared. I was desperate, and my only comfort was a song called 'Anthem' by Leonard Cohen. I'm sure if it wasn't for this beautiful song I would not have survived. It kept me going - the words were so poignant I believed he had written that song for me and that one day this nightmare would come to an end and like the message in the lyrics I would never give up hope. I listened to this song over and over.

One morning I went to the bathroom and looking in the mirror I realised my hair had gone completely white. How did that happen? I couldn't stop looking at it, my financial worries had finally taken their toll by the premature ageing of my hair. But thank goodness for those stupid douanes who were a much appreciated source of entertainment; an escape from the horrors of reality. I didn't care if they thought I was selling drugs in the shop and nothing would ever happen because I wasn't, so they could carry on wasting their resources on me as long as they wanted to.

Tom and I had been reduced to a diet of pasta and ketchup and on the odd occasion we went to Flunch, which was a self-service restaurant in Auchan Hypermarket where you could have a reasonable meal for 30 francs and then go and replenish anything apart from meat or fish, so never ending vegetables with a delicious sauce till you were full.

I had managed to avoid bumping into the Gestapo but one day a gendarme walked into the shop and presented me with my defaced driving licence, said nothing and walked out again.

We had noticed there was something strange going on with the phone at home, when we answered it or made a phone call there was a click noise and when speaking the conversation you were having would be echoing, it was very odd. One day Lorraine picked up the phone to make a call and she could hear two men having a conversation. This went on for weeks, the clicking and echoing, and we concluded that the phone was being tapped.

Over the next few weeks nothing improved but the shop was ticking over and the Boulogne Braderie was fast approaching. I tried to stock the shop as much as I could and the man from Canterbury let me have £250 worth of T-shirts and other things sale or return. On the day the weather wasn't great so we didn't put a table outside, we just opened the shop up as normal. People came and went and we did a few sales, then at 2 o'clock on the dot we were raided by the police, douanes and men in plain clothes in a conjoined effort to try and catch me with bagged up cannabis deals maybe, or a sack full of skunk, who knows.

It all happened so quickly, the police entered the shop and told everyone to leave apart from me and Tom, while the douanes searched the rails of T-shirts, the hole where we sold the smoking paraphernalia, behind the counter, in the till, on the shelves and downstairs in the basement, where we had held a few parties, and Eddie's tattoo room. A policeman stood in the doorway and told anyone who attempted to come in the shop that it was closed, while the other policemen just stood around loitering. I was not happy as we so needed those customers and they were being denied access.

Gradually the douanes were making a pile of various T-shirts and stuff from the hole and had even added my kepi and Rasta pipe to it. I asked them what they were going to do with the stuff they had chucked on the counter and was told they were taking it for evidence, so I offered them carrier bags to transport it in.

When they were satisfied there were no drugs on the premises, they gathered up the pile of things and told me to escort them to the police station. Outside the shop a crowd of onlookers had gathered to see me and my T-shirts being carted off. I don't know what the deal was between the police and the douanes but the douanes drove off in one direction, the police in another, while I walked to the police station with the two plain clothes officers who had the bags of stuff. On arrival I was told to follow one of the men to an office on the second floor and was invited to sit. Monsieur Boudin was the name of the officer who wanted to practise his English. The Sally folder arrived via another officer who decided to stay and Monsieur Boudin commenced the interview.

'We know Madame Pattinson that you are very clever' he said

'Am I'? I responded, 'in what way'?

'You know how Madame Pattinson; we know very well that you are selling cannabis in your shop'.

'That is a load of bollocks' I retorted.

Monsieur Boudin totally forgot what he was accusing me of and said 'Never mind the bollocks here's the Sex Pistols, do you like this music Madame Pattinson'?

Well what had that got to do with anything? I started to laugh at Monsieur Boudin and he went back to speaking French. He asked me about the stuff I sold in the shop, how it was encouraging young people to smoke pot and apparently before I arrived in Boulogne nobody had ever smoked cannabis. Of course they hadn't!

So he said I was going to be prosecuted for acting contrary to the 1970 Code Pénal L630 and I should get myself an avocat (barrister) as the punishment was 500,000 francs fine or 5 years in prison or both.

So that gave me something to think about, how was I going to afford an avocat and if I did get a 500,000 franc fine I had not a clue how I would pay it and the prospect of 5 years in prison didn't appeal to me either. What's more they had taken all the cannabis T-shirts which were the best sellers.

I took Monsieur Barron's advice and went to Marquise to an immobilier (estate agent) to put the house up for sale. I explained to the agent why I was selling the house and that I hadn't paid the mortgage for 18 months, we agreed it would go on the market for 600,000 francs, we had paid 710,000 francs for it and borrowed 370,000 francs, so if it sold for around 600,000 francs I would be able to pay all the debts which had been mounting up. He said he would contact Credit Agricole, the bank who had leant the money and tell them that I was going to sell it.

This time of year in the heat of the summer Phillipe would harvest his crops and at the same time we would be invaded with flies and fleas. The two cats would be host to the fleas and then as they laid their eggs on the cats the flea infestation would spread throughout the house. I tried to get rid of the fleas by spraying a product in the nooks and crannies putting a flea deterrent on the cats and dog but it didn't eradicate them. The flies we dealt with by hanging fly papers everywhere which, although they looked absolutely revolting, long yellow sticky paper strips covered in dead flies, it at least kept it under control, but the flea problem was a never-ending nightmare.

Not long after putting the house up for sale a young couple came to view it. They liked it and asked I would accept 500,000 francs, at first I thought that it wasn't enough but then I realised I didn't really have a choice if I wanted to sell it quickly.

I told the prospective buyer that I would need to find somewhere to rent and she said she had English friends who were renovating their fermette in Rety and would be looking for tenants. That sounded ideal. She said she would go and see them and let me know.

So whilst we were negotiating the house price I noticed the lady was standing on one foot and holding the other up behind her knee, she was wearing little pale pink flat canvass plimsolls and to my horror I saw that a multitude of fleas were jumping all over the foot she was standing on, then she changed feet and brushed the fleas off her foot whilst the other foot now on the ground was soon infested with more fleas. They must have been attracted to the pale pink and she didn't say a word. I didn't know what to do or say so I said nothing and ushered them out of the front door and told them to contact the agent with their offer.

Chapter 19 - Misgivings

It looked like the house was going to be sold and the English man who owned the fermette in Rety had invited me to go and visit them there and having given me directions I was on my way.

Suddenly things didn't seem so bleak, with the house being sold I could pay off the mortgage and all the utility bills that had accrued even if I was left with nothing it didn't matter.

The fermette was ideal. They still had some work to finish but they said by the time my house was sold it would be ready for me to move into. In the meantime the man and his friend offered to start moving me in by offering to take all the stuff out of the garage which husband had left there, all his power tools, a large trolley jack, socket sets, a huge tool box and two huge oak beams and four smaller bits that were meant to go under the front porch but he had never put them up. I was really grateful and they came one day in their truck and collected it all, they said it would be quite safe and be locked in one of the out-houses.

When all the contracts for the sale of the house had been drawn up for me to sign, I went happily to the immobilier, grateful that I would not be responsible for the mortgage for much longer. But my happiness was short lived. The agent told me that husband would have to present himself with his passport to sign the agreement of sale, and my heart sank. I was so near to being debt free and in an instant it had all been whisked away. I stared at the man and was on the verge of bursting into tears but I didn't want him to see that so I just thanked him and left.

After that I went to see the people with the fermette to tell them that I would not be able to move just yet and they told me it didn't matter as they had decided they were going to live in it themselves. I asked them about all my stuff in their garage and they said don't worry we'll bring it back. But they never did and I guess that's all they wanted - just to steal my stuff that I could have sold for us.

I went and told Monsieur Barron what had happened and he said unfortunately if the things were on their property and I had no proof that any of it was mine I could do absolutely nothing about it. So that was that! I had pretty much aided and abetted a robbery of my own stuff to a couple of thieving reprobates.

There was one problem after another. One of the back lights on the van had stopped working and I had to change it or else I would have the Gestapo or the gendarmes on motorbikes chasing me. So I went and bought a replacement and asked one of Monsieur Van Pepperstraaten's customers to change it for me. All was well till I drove the van and everything was wrong; when I indicated right the left indicator flashed and if I indicated left the right indicator flashed; when I put my foot on the brake the headlights lit up. Everything I tried to do resulted in disaster. Was it just me or was it things that were just out of my control? I wondered how much more could go wrong,

In just a few weeks we'd been infested with fleas and flies, I couldn't sell the house because of a technical hitch, I'd been robbed right under my nose and now my headlights came on when I applied the brake pedal. I had a motto that tomorrow would be better than today because it couldn't get any worse. Living in hope was good, but I would probably die in despair.

We struggled on through the summer and did go to Lille for the braderie but it wasn't great and the sales were down on the previous two years. There was very little stock in the shop and the man from Canterbury was asking for his money and had said he would have to come and take his T-shirts back if I couldn't pay him.

And sadly that's what he did do, reducing our stock to just a few T-shirts that we hadn't been able to sell over the last few months. But I am a true believer that when all seems lost there is always something or someone that will come to the rescue and it did! I had met a man in Monsieur Van Pepperstraaten's café one day who had something to do with a charity that dealt in second hand clothes and he said he would bring some over from England that I could sell in the shop and that could keep us going for a little while.

The following week he turned up with suitcases and huge bags of clothes and they were decent clothes, there were several fur coats in amongst it all. I was so grateful to this man and we were able to stock the shop for a while longer. Three weeks later he returned again with more clothes for us to sell.

With no hope of selling the house or paying the mortgage I wondered how we could possibly go on living there. For the moment we were, but I worried that we would be thrown out and have nowhere to go. Twice when we had come home there had been notices stuck on the front door that bailiffs had called, so they were closing in on us but I was not going to be intimidated, I was going to carry on to the bitter end come what may, in hope that a miracle might happen.

Winter was upon us and I feared how we would get through it. Sometimes when we arrived home there would be a pile of logs Phillipe the farmer had left outside for us, or my neighbour Edith would leave a container of her homemade soup. I was very grateful for these kind gestures.

I had little hope but as a last resort I plucked up enough courage to go to the Banque de France which happened to be in Place d'Angleterre in Boulogne and ask to borrow 5000f which would have at least paid something off the electricity bill and water rates. I went to the bank one morning, and it was difficult to gain entry as there was an intercom system on which you had to say who you were before a switch was released and you could go in, but once in I took my place at the end of the queue. French banks were very open, with no bullet proof glass between the customer and bank clerk. I glanced around at the décor and the people waiting patiently for their turn. When at last I arrived at the counter I had barely opened my mouth to speak when the bank clerk shouted at the top of her voice for all the customers to hear, 'get out of here you are a bad payer'. I looked behind me hoping she was shouting at someone else but she was glaring at me. I looked her in the eye and pointed to myself as if I was questioning her remark was aimed at me and she nodded. There was no choice but to leave as quickly as possible without looking at any of the customers who had just heard those unkind words. I turned away and headed for the door, but it was harder to get out than in, I guess to stop thieves escaping. I was feeling so embarrassed it felt like an eternity before the door opened and let me out to fresh air and freedom. I knew it was a bad idea.

Shortly after this I received two letters which arrived at the shop and I had to sign for both of them. The first letter was from a man called Pascal Ruffin who was a Mandataire Judiciare (Judicial Agent) inviting me to his office in Place D'Angleterre, the second letter was from the Palace de Justice Boulogne-sur-Mer giving me the date of my court case which was March 13th. 1997.

I would need a lawyer if I was facing the possibility of five years in prison and I was not hopeful that I would find such a lawyer in Boulogne. We sometimes sold a controversial magazine called L'Elephant Rose which promoted the consumption of cannabis and the ideals of free sex. This magazine had been subject to a great deal of legal action but whether it was legal or illegal it had managed to publish every month despite the harassment from the French authorities. It often had stories of people who had been in trouble for possession or selling cannabis and avocats who had represented these people won their case and they had walked free from the court. We got hold of a copy of L'Elephant Rose and searched for names of avocats who were all based in Paris. I chose a man called Monsieur Fabien Costello, an avocat with a good record of keeping cannabis offenders out of prison, so I contacted Monsieur Costello, whose office was right in the centre of Paris, and made an appointment to see him.

I went to see Pascal Ruffin first. I had an idea what he was going to tell me and I was right, Credit Agricole had written to the courts saying I owed them three years mortgage and they wanted their money back, and who could blame them, we had been living in the house for nothing since January 1994 and Pascal Ruffin was going to put me, my house, the shop and all my possessions into liquidation. The immediate prospects were looking bleak; homeless, jobless, penniless, destitute and a life of penury. Maybe five years in prison wasn't such a bad idea after all! At least I'd have a roof over my head and be fed three times a day, but what of Tom and Lorraine? No, I was not giving up in my plight to overcome the misery husband had unmercifully inflicted upon us.

The journey to Paris for my appointment with Fabien Costello was fine till I got to Paris and then I had to take the metro. I'm useless in big cities and totally out of my comfort zone but he had given me instructions and I did find him. Fabien Costello greeted me and seemed in a hurry, he had a tanned intelligent face, very dark eyes and a terrific beak of a nose but still a handsome man. As he stood up from behind his desk I noticed how terribly short he was and dwarfed by my 5' 3".

I told him about the harassment I had suffered from the douanes and the amount of times they had had me in their office at Boulogne Port, the raid on the shop and the stuff they had taken. He took notes and told me he would drive to Boulogne for the hearing and his fee was 5000 francs in advance, then said he had another appointment somewhere else and bundled me out of his office, I had been there for half an hour and then made my way back to Boulogne via the metro and the TGV.

On my return journey I hatched a plan on how to pay the avocat, not all but a good part of it.

Chapter 20 - A Means to an End

The letter box at the end of the drive had so much mail stuffed into it that letters had started to ooze out of the bottom, and the bailiffs were closing in fast. The first thing they would take was the van, not worth very much but probably the biggest asset apart from the log burner which was attached to the house and was hopefully not eligible for seizure for that reason.

The van, although falling to bits, had a super engine in it and so I decided that I would try and sell the engine and the bailiffs could take the van without realising it had no engine in it.

Lorraine's current boyfriend Nico, the guitarist from Liebemachnr who had played at Rockstock 2, had invited us to eat with him and his parents who lived in Pont Brique just outside Boulogne. Serge and Liliane were such nice people and we had a fabulous meal for the first time in ages. Serge had a friend who was a car mechanic and he said he would ask his friend if he would like to buy the engine from me.

Serge's friend soon came to look at the engine and said he would give me 2500 francs for it, but then I would be car-less which wasn't so great.

I contacted my friend in Hastings who had fixed the brakes on the van when I had taken the 14 fans to Tom's concert and asked him if he knew anyone with an old banger for sale for not more than £50. It wouldn't need an MOT as they wouldn't know if it had one or not in France. He knew someone with an old Maestro and said he would get it for me and I would have to meet him in Dover to collect it. I asked him to bring a new number plate for my new car.

Serge's friend came round with a colleague to our house one day and removed the engine from the van, and so the van was now stuck on the driveway waiting for the bailiffs. Serge took us to Boulogne and we took the Seacat to Dover to collect the Maestro. So with no MOT, tax or insurance I was once again mobile with my new car and its new registration number SAL1E, which we stuck on with super glue.

I had half the money to pay for my avocat all I needed was another 2500francs.

I was summonsed to Maître Ruffin's office again and to bring my debts with me so as to start the procedure of the liquidation of my assets. I was still fearful of opening the letter box so I just pulled two envelope that were sticking out of the bottom. I had no idea how old these bills were. I was feeling quite apprehensive about this meeting as I knew it was the beginning of the end so I smoked a large joint to relax me and give me courage.

By the time I reached Maître Ruffin's office I was completely stoned. I thought I was going to his office but instead I was led into a different room with a high ceiling and not much furniture in it. I saw before me a huge round table with men sitting around it, there were thirteen in all and they were wearing black cloaks and large floppy black berets, they reminded me of a flock of crows and I didn't know what to make of them. This was a strange situation. I felt as if I had changed centuries and gone backwards about 300 years. Maître Ruffin, who was also wearing the same outfit as the others, told me to sit down next to him on the only vacant seat. I felt uncomfortable and they looked ridiculous; why were they wearing those strange outfits just for me. Then Maître Ruffin asked me if I had brought my bills with me and I handed him the two envelopes I had pulled out of the letter box, 'is this all you have' he asked, 'no, I haven't opened the letter box for months' I told him 'I am afraid to'. He looked at me kindly and told me I needn't be afraid anymore and he was going to take care of my affairs from now on. I was not to pay any bills or if I did I could go to prison. That was a great relief, mustn't pay any bills; if I do I will go to prison. I wanted to laugh, what sort of a law was that? I was handed a form to sign which said I agreed that Maître Ruffin could proceed with the liquidation and sale by public auction of my material assets and he told me that from now on my mail would be redirected to his office.

I told him I didn't have any assets apart from the house which I hadn't paid any mortgage on for nearly four years. He asked me if I had a till in the shop. I said I had and he asked me to bring it to his office when the meeting had finished.

If that was all I had to sacrifice, my house and the till I guessed that wasn't too much to suffer. So I was allowed to leave, I went to the shop and emptied the few centimes that were still in the till. There were only a few garments that were left from the kind man from the charity hanging on the nearly bare rails, and a few bits and pieces in the glass counter in the hole. It was the end of the Malice shop. I sat in it for a while waiting for the cannabis to wear off, then carried the till back round to Maître Ruffin's office.

It didn't take long for the Gestapo to catch me in my new car with false number plates. I just kept telling him that I couldn't afford to change my driving licence yet but I would, and begged him not to do anything drastic against me. It worked and each time he gave me a warning that I had to change my licence in the next two weeks or he would ban me from driving the next time.

Eventually, just before Christmas, the shop closed for the last time and I handed the keys back to the agent. Things had been so bad that I had only been able to put 10 francs worth of petrol in the car each day to get to Boulogne and back.

We did not celebrate Christmas. I couldn't even buy my children a Christmas present.

Things could get no worse. We were at rock bottom and the only way now was up.

Chapter 21 - New Year New Beginnings

Thank God for good people! Phillipe was supplying us with a regular pile of logs he cut from his woods and Edith our neighbour supplied us with soup.

New Year's Eve we were invited to a soirée in Wideham, a small village just outside Etaples where there was a band playing in a little restaurant and bar owned by a man called Pierrot who loved music, wine, cooking and cannabis. Pierrot was a lovely cool, chilled out, fun loving man in his mid-50's and had long grey curly hair and a set of floor standing bongo drums which he regularly played to his customers.

This night was so cold and the temperature had dropped to -15 degrees and everything was frozen solid including my Maestro. Having seen the new year in, it was time to go but my car was going nowhere, it wouldn't start as it probably didn't have any anti-freeze in it, so Guillaume the singer in the band Black Dust drove us the 43 kilometres home in freezing icy conditions in his Peugeot 106 leaving my Maestro at Pierrot's restaurant.

The next day Serge turned up at Wierre Effroy having been informed of the frozen Maestro by Sebastien, his youngest son, who had been at Pierrot's party. It was still bitterly cold and the plan was to tow the Maestro to the top of a very steep hill on the way out of Wideham and then try to bump start it on the way down. Serge towed us to the top of the hill, got in to the Maestro, and Tom and I pushed the car to the start of the steep descent and with one mighty shove it started to roll slowly down the hill, we watched Serge till he disappeared round a bend still freewheeling not knowing that Tom had left his stash of cannabis in the door panel. We sat in Serge's car waiting for his return, and a good half hour later we saw the roof of the Maestro came triumphantly back up the hill with Serge looking pleased with himself, proud of his accomplishment. We went to Pierrot's bar for a celebratory drink paid for by Serge.

Whilst there I met Pierrot's girlfriend, an English lady called Susan who owned a bar come hotel in Condette, a village not far away from Wideham where Le Château d'Hardelot stood in all its splendour. I told Susan how desperate I was for a job and she said she had been working in Eastenders, a beer and wine warehouse in Calais, for a man called Dave West who had made millions of pounds selling beer and wine extremely cheaply, and although she no longer worked for him she felt sure he would give me a job. She gave me directions on how to find it. I was so grateful for the information and it seemed there was a glimmer of hope at last.

The next day with very little petrol I drove off to Calais to find Eastenders on an industrial estate called Marcel Doret, Junction 3. It was a huge warehouse and there were palettes of wine everywhere. Dave West was not there and an employee phoned him and I was sent to his house which was down in the old port of Calais, an area of neglected large empty buildings and train tracks. I found his house and was quite shocked at the state of it for someone who was a multi-millionaire. The windows were broken, and dirty old net curtains were flapping through them in the wind or caught on the jagged edges of the broken glass; there was a large ripped Union Jack attached to a drainpipe flapping about.

I knocked on the pale green door with the paint peeling off it, and a short chubby man with very tight curly hair tied back in a ponytail answered, with a fierce looking Belgian Shepherd by his side called Shanty. Dave West invited me into his house, and I asked him if the dog was vicious; he told me not to look at it as it had bitten people before and had recently killed a cat in the warehouse. There were stacked up papers everywhere 3 to 4 foot high and hardly any space to walk. I was terrified of the dog and fearful of tripping over the mess I was having to climb over. We went down a staircase which had piles of papers on every step and arrived in the basement, which was dark and dingy and filthy and stank of cigarette smoke. There were empty cigarette packets all over the floor with Eastenders written on them and a picture of Dave West on the front.

The Dave West cigarettes

How could a man with all his money live in such a disgusting state? And he was married, his wife was called Kath and she sold cigarettes and tobacco in Adinkirke the first village over the border into Belgium. I told him I was desperate for a job and he said that he only employed 'desperadoes', he paid 200 francs a day or he could give me £20 whichever I preferred, and he would pay me daily; the hours were 8 a.m. to 8 p.m. and a twenty minute lunch break six days a week. I could start the following week. I was so happy he had saved my life and I would show my gratitude by working really hard. I wanted to get out of his house - I didn't like being there and I didn't like the dog and I wanted to get home and tell Tom the good news.

Having a job at Eastenders was such a relief I felt a great weight had been lifted and I couldn't wait to start.

I arrived bright and early the following Monday and was put to work with a French girl called Marlène who was young and very pretty with long naturally blond hair to her waist. She spoke perfect English. She showed me how to use a pump truck and manoeuvre palettes of wine from one aisle to another. Everything was dusty and when we pulled the pallets out of the line there were always rat droppings underneath. The beer was stored at the far end of the warehouse - row upon row of palettes of beer stacked 4 high.

Eastenders was the coldest place I had ever worked in; the front shutter which spanned a good 20 feet was broken and was stuck open and the back door was permanently open for the comings and goings of the forklift trucks unloading the delivery lorries and loading them up with empty pallets. The wind whistled through the building and I could see my breath. No matter how much clothing, scarves and woolly hats I wore I was always perished and gloves made no difference either.

I gradually got to meet the other staff members, Bubbs from Dagenham with long wavy hair and a strong cockney accent was a forklift driver, John from Bethnal Green a forklift and lorry driver, Paul from Glasgow a forklift driver, Sammi from Morocco the front of house man, Frank from Calais the security guard, Mad Tim, I don't know where he came from but he looked like the singer from Prodigy with a hellish temper that led to crying like a child after a tantrum, Nigel who always had a bottle of Bacardi in his pocket and was swigging it all day long. There were a couple of nice English girls in the office, one a wine buyer and the other a secretary, and there was Andrew the accountant. And it was true all these people working on the floor were desperadoes, all working for a pittance and I was one of them.

The work was hard and relentless, I was fearful of getting the sack if I wasn't quick enough or strong enough. Lunch break was quick, the first day I didn't have any because I had nothing to bring but there was a place round the corner called Pidou that sold burgers and bacon sandwiches and biscuits if you wanted to go there. On Sundays the boss would go out and come back with roast chickens or pizzas for the staff.

People in white vans otherwise known as 'the white van brigade' would come and buy palettes of beer and wine to take back to England and sell cheaply, undercutting the price of off licences and supermarkets. Dave West had his own brand of lager called ESP and sold it in the little dumpy bottles, a pack of 24 for £4.00. I soon realised that Eastenders was the hub of the 'booze cruise' era; 24-hour non-stop trading of beer and wine, hundreds of thousands of pounds worth of merchandise selling by the hour.

After a few weeks Tom also started to work at Eastenders as a forklift driver and, instructed by Bubbs, he was soon whizzing up and down the aisles at great speed. I had been moved onto the checkout, so with calculator in one hand you would add up all the cases of beer and wine on the huge trolleys and the palettes of beer taken out to the vans on the forklifts. It was a bit daunting at first but once I'd done it a few times I learnt the prices and those I didn't I guessed. After the checkout job I was promoted to the honour of taking the money at the till behind bullet proof glass with an open area to speak through and where the money was paid. The first day in the till I was shown by Dave West how to use the money counting machine which would count the £50, £20 and £10 pound notes into wads of one thousand pounds and then we would put a money band round the wad and shove it through a hole at the back of the room into Dave West's counting parlour. After that he showed me two loaded guns, one on a shelf at the front just above your head and the other to the right just sitting there, which I was expected to use if anyone ever tried to steal or rob any property belonging to the establishment.

The first time I was working on the till more than £100,000 must have passed through my hands. I had never handled so much money in my life.

Over the following months I had various jobs at Eastenders and learnt things that both amazed and shocked me.

Some evenings John used to go out in the lorry with a set of bolt-croppers to the other supermarkets to cut the chains of the trolleys (which were otherwise detached by inserting a 10 franc coin into the trolley) and bring them back to Eastenders for Dave West's customers to use.

One busy Sunday when I was checking out the trolleys and Dave West was on the till, an elderly man had been and paid for his shopping and presently he came back pushing his empty supermarket trolley. He asked Dave West if he would give him 10 francs as there were no more trolleys outside to plug into his to return his 10 francs. To my horror and embarrassment Dave West retorted by sniffing loudly and wiping his nose with the back of his hand and shouted at this poor little man 'I wouldn't give you the fucking pickings out of me nose, now fuck off'. I didn't have one either or I would have given it to the bewildered little man.

There were two other establishments which were part of Eastenders, a smaller warehouse a few streets away and a shop on the outskirts of Calais. On the odd occasion I would be sent to work in the other warehouse and noticed there were always several bin liners full of unopened tobacco pouches. I asked why they were there but I never got an answer. One day I was there alone with Nigel who was a bit the worse for wear so I asked him why all this lose tobacco was packed in bin bags. He told me that Dave West had an agreement with the police and the deal was that when his customers had filled their white vans with beer and wine they would drive up to Adinkirke to the warehouse run by Dave West's wife to buy boxes of cigarettes and tobacco, and in the meantime Dave West would take the registration numbers of the vehicles and pass it on to the police who in turn would stop the van on their return journey and confiscate all the cigarettes and tobacco, keeping half for themselves, and return the other half of the haul to Eastenders then back to Adinkirke to be sold on again. This deal with the police ensured that Dave West would not be harassed by them for any other illegal antics he might and most probably was involved in.

Chapter 22 - In the Bleak Mid-Winter

It was February and the temperature had plummeted to minus 15 degrees like it had at New Year and the super glue which we had stuck the false number plates on with had gone brittle and the back number plate had fallen off and so I had chucked it in the boot. I had been ducking and diving trying to avoid the Gestapo, then one day I had parked in the car park of Champion, a small Supermarket in Boulogne, and when I got back to my car the Gestapo was waiting for me. I could not get away so I had to face him. He told me that it was illegal to drive a car with no number plate so I tried to reassure him that although he couldn't see it, it was safe in the boot and I opened it to prove it to him. He said I had to put it back in its rightful place or I would be in serious trouble so I told him it was a false number plate, but he said he didn't care and I must put it back. 'OK I'll do that' I promised. He seemed to have forgotten about the illegal driving licence.

The car was frozen solid and wouldn't start in the mornings and we had to be at work for 8 o'clock. I was fearful of getting the sack and dared not be late. Phillipe came to the rescue once again, every morning we had to push the car down his long driveway our hands on the verge of frostbite by the time we got there. He attached a rope from the car to the back of his tractor, then he drove round and round the yard until the frozen engine burst into life. This was the only way to start the car and it became part of our daily routine for the duration of the cold weather.

The court case was looming and the possibility I could go to prison for 5 years was daunting. I hadn't heard from the avocat Fabien Costello but I could only hope that he would turn up and convince the judge that I hadn't done anything wrong.

Dave West had condescended in giving me and Tom the day off to attend my court case.

Thursday 13th March 1997, I arrived at the Palais de Justice Boulogne sur Mer, a grey, cold and windy day. I had dressed in black leggings, a little black fluffy jumper and a short knubby black jacket and of course my Doc Martens.

I had been waiting for my lawyer in the huge stone gallery for twenty minutes and I feared he wasn't going to turn up. It smelt of old cigarette smoke and people, and there was a group of men standing together talking but he wasn't among them. Presently my friend Mary came up the huge stone staircase. She had come to give me moral support and I was so pleased to see her. We stood by one of the large windows that looked out onto the Place de la Résistance, there was five minutes to go before the afternoon session was going to begin, then suddenly there he was hurrying across the square, his beige rain coat billowing in the cold breeze blowing directly off the Channel. He dashed into the hall and hustled us upstairs, gabbling to me in French, but he was speaking so quickly I didn't understand what he was saying. Luckily Mary spoke French fluently and translated for me.

We went into the court room and settled down on a hard wooden bench. The court room had beautiful high ceilings with plaster work picked out in pale apple green and white, the walls also green and white. The judge's bench all dark wood and was set up on a platform with a large dark wooden throne set in the centre. To the left was a special little platform holding a one-seater bench for the 'Procureur de le République' the state's representative, while to the right opposite the Procureur was another little platform exactly the same for 'Le Greffier', the court clerk whose job was to note the judge's remarks.

My lawyer swept majestically down the central aisle and placed himself on the cushioned benches, and looked around the court room where presently a procession of men appeared from a side door wearing black silk robes, some with fur on the ends of their scarves and some without, joined him. I noticed that one of them was Maître Baron, the British Consul.

We sat sucking Fisherman's Friends, then suddenly Tom and my fan club crowded into the court room with their nose-rings, earrings, Mohican hair styles, tattoos and wearing appropriate clothing which they had purchased from the Malice shop.

Then a bell rang out and in swept the judge with his chorus line of two young women also robed in black silk. He sat in his high backed throne and the two women, one either side, were hidden from view behind stacks of files some 6 inches thick.

The judge started by doling out sentences for cases he had heard two weeks previously. He spoke in such a low monotone that we could hardly hear what he was saying while our bums where becoming positively numb from the hardness of our seat.

The Judge proceeded to read out the accusations, a man had been shooting protected species of wild birds with a gun but no licence, the next was an Englishman in handcuffs who had been caught drug-running, he received a three year prison sentence, five years forbidden to step foot in France and a 1,600,000 franc fine (£160,000). Then a man who had a sexual relationship with a minor got a five-year prison sentence and a 1000 franc fine and so it continued until the remaining defendants were tried and sentenced.

At last the sentencing finished and the trials got under way.

Four gypsy men who had been selling carpets without prices marked on them, at markets, braderies and hired halls and sticking adverts on lamp posts, and as they did not have a 'Carte de Commerce', a shopkeeper had made a complaint to the Union.

The lawyers droned on, one for the sellers and one for The Union of Shopkeepers, none other than the Franco-British Maître Baron.

As the voices droned on the judge sat turning a large calendar round and round. He was a tall, thin, pale man with a rigid mouth and pale tired eyes behind glasses. His greying hair stood on end and he seemed miles away fiddling endlessly with his calendar.

The 'Procureur' was small and slightly plump with a pink face and short mousy hair, and he also wore a bored look and fidgeted as much as the judge. Once the legal arguments had finished the judge said he would pass sentence on 27th. March.

Then it was my turn. It was four o'clock. I was called and my well-wishers wished me good luck as I walked to the front of the courtroom. The Judge's bench reached nearly to the top of my head and I felt dwarfed by this huge piece of furniture before me.

The judge read out the charges against me which were 'selling equipment which would incite the use of drugs'. He then asked me what I had to say, so having been told what to say by my lawyer and which was only the truth, I said that I sold these things in my shop as I hoped they would sell well, that the goods were not illegal in

France or elsewhere and I had bought the goods from an authorised wholesaler and that I had paid VAT on all of it and it was open and above board. The judge told me to sit down and my lawyer stood up. He swished his robe behind him and swept forward, and began to speak in a ringing, actor type voice with rapid, staccato speech. He didn't mention me but launched into the reason why there was no case. According to him the case should have been brought by the 'Procureur' under Clause L680 instead of Clause L630 which had been mistakenly used. He said he couldn't defend his client because the drug squad hadn't been notified and that everything had been taken on hearsay and imaginings by the police and customs. Also the so-called proof had been destroyed before the trial which was forbidden under the law and he gave the number of the article to prove it. He also stated that only the Procureur of Boulogne sur Mer brought such badly presented cases before the court and that I had suffered harassment over a long period of time from the police and douanes.

While he had been talking the Judge had sat up straighter and forgot about his calendar. His eyes had become wide like organ stops. At the same time the 'Procureur' who had been pink faced became healthily red.

The judge interrupted the proceedings and left the courtroom accompanied by the 'Procureur', Greffier' and his assistants. Obviously, they had not expected this and went off to consult their law books. They were out for a long 15 minutes and I chatted to an Englishman in handcuffs and my lawyer paced up and down swishing his robe and looking thoughtful. Then the Judge and his entourage came back and everyone stood and then sat down again. The judge announced that the trial would take place on its original basis and that my lawyer would have to accept it. He looked angry at my Parisian lawyer coming here and laying down the law.

The judge then proceeded to look at the evidence he did have and none of it was the merchandise they had seized from the shop, that had disappeared. All he had was my kepi with the 'Smoke Pot' patch on the front, the long stemmed Rasta pipe and one t-shirt that had an inconsequential leaf design on it. I explained that the kepi was mine to wear and the pipe didn't draw and wasn't smokable. I had bought both for myself at a braderie in Etaples. He asked me to explain the leaves on the t-shirt and I replied that they could be cannabis or hemp which was from the same plant, but whatever they were meant to be they were badly drawn and cannabis leaves had 7 lobes on them and these only had 5. Then the Judge asked me how many times the police and douanes had visited me or complained about my merchandise I told him thirty-three times. Everyone in the room gasped with shock. Then a policeman standing at the back said aloud that it wasn't true and Tom pitched up that it was true and we had the dates.

Then the 'Procureur' stood up and tried to make his case against me. He stated that before I had opened the Malice shop nobody in Boulogne had ever smoked cannabis. My merchandise of which none was in the courtroom, although they did have a small album of photos taken by the police was an invitation to take drugs. He said that if a minor were to buy a t-shirt with a cannabis leaf design on it, he would be sure to say to himself when he got home 'Now I've got the gear, maybe I should try the drug' he carried on in this vein but I knew that he had been thrown off balance by my lawyer saying at the beginning that he didn't really have a case. Once he sat down, he put his hand against his face for the rest of the trial and hid himself from our view.

Then the judge showed me the photo album and asked me to explain each photo. The photo of the Rasta man lying on a lawn smoking a joint I explained by telling him that in England when the grass grew too long to be cut by a mower people tended to burn it. I tried to justify each photo but by the time we got to the t-shirt with a picture of the Pope saying 'I Like the Pope he Smokes Dope' I had run out of all reasonable excuses, so I said I guessed that one must be telling the truth. Everyone in the courtroom was murmuring that they hadn't made much of a case against me.

Then it was the turn of Fabien Costello my lawyer.

I could see he was enjoying himself on centre stage with his Parisian airs swooping up and down dramatically saying how we should forbid pop songs, including the Beatles, because they might incite the taking of drugs. He said that SEITA should be sued (the French tobacco monopoly controlling the sale of tobacco in France and handing the heavy duty tax over to the government), because they sold cigarette rolling equipment and papers which could be used for drugs. We should forbid people for smoking pipes because they might be used for drugs instead of tobacco. Then he swooped upon his briefcase and took out a very serious, often political magazine with a cover picture of a couple smoking joints and asked the Procureur to prosecute them for inciting the use of drugs.

He ended with a swirl of his robe as he returned to his place on the bench. The Procureur stood up and asked for a fine of 5,000 francs against me. The Judge said sentence would be handed out on the 27th March.

We all left the courtroom and met my lawyer in the stone gallery outside. We all lit up our cigarettes and puffed with relief. The lawyer was quite satisfied; he knew the Procureur had been ready to ask for a prison sentence and a hefty fine because if he could have proved that I had been inciting young people to take drugs, it is considered a serious crime. The very fact that he had asked for such a small fine showed that he knew his case had been very badly prepared and that he didn't have much of anything to hold against me.

Fabien Costello took his leave and went to drive the long journey back to Paris with only half his money I had from the sale of the van engine. I said I would send him the rest when I had it. Even if I had been able to pay him the full amount of 5,000 francs, he had been worth it.

Chapter 23 - The Sentence

The morning of March 27th dawned blustery and grey. I had arranged to meet Mary half an hour before the afternoon session began but there was no sign of her. Eventually I spotted Mary desperately searching for a parking spot and in the end she reversed up a one-way street to the only empty space. We hugged and went up the cracked stone staircase into the Palais de Justice, I was nervous and trying to hide it was not easy. I had decided to wear a short tight denim dress with black tights and of course my Doc Martens. We climbed the two twisting flights of stairs to the upper gallery where groups of people wandered around in their robes and wigs carrying bundles of folders and papers.

The time came for us to enter the courtroom, which was full of hand-cuffed people, police, lawyers and the public. We found a space on the same hard wooden benches we had sat on before and I noticed the green-faced clock had stopped at 4 o'clock. I also spotted the Procureur sat there in his civvies and another black-robed servant of the peace was sitting on his high wooden perch. I thought that he had probably turned up to see what was going to happen to me and Tom sitting a few rows back from us, and remarked on the expensive sweater he was wearing. The four gypsies, who had been done for the dodgy carpet selling and were sat behind us muttering in foreign tongues, had turned up to receive their sentence too. Then suddenly a bell started to toll to signal that the judge was on his way, we all stood and in he walked stoop-shouldered with an incomplete harem, his assistants today are a man and a woman both heavily loaded with fat files, it was like the beginning of some weird theatrical performance and I found the strange public presentation being acted out in front of me highly amusing. The judge, mumbling, began to dish out sentences - all lengths of imprisonment and different sized fines, then it was the dodgy carpet people, they got a huge fine and had all their carpets confiscated, which would be sold at a public auction. One of the gypsies stood up and complained about the carpets being publicly auctioned and the judge informed him that he had the right to appeal against the sentence. So on that note the gypsies got up and trooped out of the courtroom muttering to themselves.

I had been left till last, and all the hand-cuffed prisoners sat up straight when my name and crime were read out. I made my way to the front of the high bench where the Judge sat looking down on me. He announced that part of my case had been abandoned since the proof had been destroyed, which pleased me, so he could only judge on the effects he had been given at the hearing, for which I was found guilty as charged and he imposed a 5000 franc fine. As for the kepi and Smoke Pot patch, it would be retained and destroyed. The T-shirt with the Rasta man he made a joke about. As for the pipe, he said he had looked closely at the pipe and had found that it resembled the ones made in the Haute Savoie (Alps) area. Some people put them on their walls as decoration, so I could have it back. I told him he could keep it as a souvenir and to my surprise he smiled at me and announced he could not accept bribery as he wasn't a judge in Marseille! I then bravely asked him how I was meant to pay the fine and he suddenly became benevolent and said I could pay it in instalments.

I wished him good day and turned to go back to where we had been sitting and to my surprise all the prisoners sitting in hand-cuffs started clapping and smiling. I felt like a star leaving this grand stage of comedy.

I had one more undertaking to carry out, one final act of defiance for the douanes to put closure on the previous three years of them chasing me in the hope of catching me in possession of a load of cannabis with the intention to sell. They had been so wrong, as I had never sold any kind of drug in my life and I had no intention of doing so. Shortly after the sentence at the Palais de Justice where at least one of them had been present I drove down to the port and went into the office where I had spent so much time. Luckily there were four or five douaniers inside. I didn't bother speaking to them, I turned my back and did a moony at them exposing the tattoo of the stoned douanier on my left buttock and they all roared with laughter. One asked me if it was their colleague Daniel there on my cheek, I said it was all of them as I hoisted my French knickers and leggings back up. I bade them a fond farewell and for the last time I left.

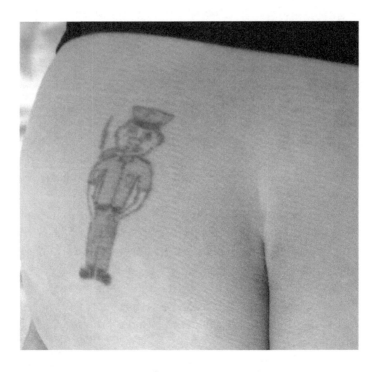

The moony

Chapter 24 - A Sense of Closure

Shortly after the sentence, I was back in the same courtroom being made bankrupt, this time by a different judge, which meant that any debts I had accrued before that date would be shelved, which I supposed would include the 5000 franc fine which I had just been presented with; whether it did or did not I never paid it and never heard any more about it. Husband was ordered to pay 2500 francs per month to go towards Tom's keep and studies but of course it was a fruitless demand as he had no idea I had divorced him and no one knew where he was anyway.

So our lives consisted of the same gruelling routine, working 12 hours a day 6 days a week and struggling to live on the pittance (which we received in coins daily) that Dave West begrudgingly paid us for our hard work.

One day however the routine changed.

A little Scottish fella called Paul had been employed as a forklift driver and for some reason or other Dave West had sacked him. We were all quite sad as Paul was a nice chap and quite normal as staff there went. It was around 11 o'clock and the warehouse was busy with customers and all of a sudden there was a thick cloud of black smoke billowing along the roof of the building heading towards the broken front entrance. We quickly ushered the customers to safety and the boys on the forklifts in the back where the fire was were moving the pallets outside as quickly as they could. Mad Tim came charging through the doors from the staff quarters carrying 7 heavy fire extinguishers and nearly on his knees with the weight, heading towards the fire which was now well alight. There was a real danger of us burning to death or being run over by the cavalcade of forklift trucks. Bottles of wine were exploding and cans of beer were flying all over the place from the pressure of the heat. There were some customers who refused to leave so in the end I pulled their trolley away and pushed them outside. The pandemonium lasted a good 15 minutes and by the time the fire brigade arrived the fire was pretty much under control. It was deemed that sacked Scottish Paul had retaliated by putting a petrol soaked rag in an empty bottle of ESP and chucked it up onto the pallets which had then fallen down to the ground in between and that's why it had taken a couple of hours to take hold.

It took us three days to clear up the mess, which was on biblical proportions, and we all ruined our boots walking on the mountains of broken glass which tore the soles to smithereens. I asked Dave West if he would buy me a new pair of boots and he said if he did that then everybody would want new boots. I was very angry, but needed my job too much to kick up a fuss..

The house that was meant to have been full of hope and prospects of a wonderful new life was now just a shattered dream and was going to be auctioned off for the bank to try and retrieve some of its lost money. The process of auctioning a repossessed house in France is long and painful. Three candles are lit and the public start bidding on the property and when the third candle is extinguished the highest bidder wins.

Changes were taking place and we had to look for somewhere else to live. I had had a string of old bangers that would drive for a few months and then die, and at this moment in time I owned a Ford Sierra that was flesh and rust coloured. It was beset with problems from the day it arrived from the UK, brought over by a friend, and cost £80 of which I could only offer £40.

Within days of having it we were going to work one morning in the pouring rain when the windscreen wiper fell off my side and I had to hold the broken wiper and clear the windscreen manually and my arm got soaked. We got to work and Little Dave, Dave West's eldest son, re-attached the snapped off wiper by tying it back on with string to whatever it had broken off of. And for a time it stayed on there because it didn't rain, and when it did all was well for a while. I was going home after my 12 hour shift and just as I got onto the dual carriageway I could smell burning but I ignored it until I saw smoke billowing out of the bonnet just below the windscreen. I pulled in and opened the bonnet to see the string that was holding the wiper on was on fire, caused by the friction of the motor. Luckily I had half a bottle of water that I chucked on it to put it out.

The next day I stopped off in Marquise at the only garage to buy a new wiper and he only had one which he said it was not really meant for my make of car but he attached it anyway. I think it was meant for a lorry as it stuck out 2 inches off the side of the windscreen.

The Sierra had all sorts of problems and currently it was an electrical one so if it rained the electrics would stop working. One night on the way home from work it was pouring with rain with gale force winds. I was dreading coming off the dual carriageway because I knew if I had to stop the engine would cut out and I would never get going again. Just as I got to the junction to turn left I could see the blurred headlights of another car coming from the right, so I had no choice but to stop and so did the engine and that was that; there I was broken down at the road junction in a storm several miles from home. I couldn't push the car anywhere so I just sat there snivelling. Although the hazard lights were flashing, cars were still pulling up behind me thinking I was going to move, but I wasn't and I just did not know what to do. I sat there for a good hour and the storm was still raging, when all of a sudden the passenger door opened and a man got in. I was surprised to hear him speak with an English accent. He realised I had broken down and told me to open the bonnet which I did, and he was out there in the wind and rain holding the bonnet open trying to see what the problem was. He went to get his friends and they pushed my car to a safer place on the side of the road and offered me a lift home. I was scared but had no choice but to accept their offer, so clutching my box of broken bits of pallet for the fire I reluctantly got into the back of their car which had no back doors. They said they were painters on their way back from Holland and asked if they could stay the night at home. I had to agree as they were taking me home. When we got inside I took a good look at my three rescuers. One had a broken nose which was flat against his face apart from the end bit where his nostrils were. I thought they were artists but then noticed they were all wearing white overalls implying they were painters and decorators not artists. I offered them my dinner which was a few rashers of bacon and some eggs. There wasn't enough for four people so I went without. One of them lit the log burner and they seemed quite nice men but I was still terrified. I went to bed as soon as I could and crept into Tom's room to get an old Marshall speaker to put behind my bedroom door as there were no locks, and I took the cricket bat to bed with me. I think they knew I was frightened as none of them came upstairs to use the bathroom. I could hear them going into the garden for a pee. The next day the weather was calm and they drove me back to my abandoned car. One guy got in and it started straight away. He said the wind had dried it out. I thanked them and drove off to work, relieved I was still alive.

I put up with the old Sierra breaking down every so often but it was better than nothing and lasted till the next old banger.

Tom's band Malice in Wonderland had split up and Tom and Arno had gone to play for Marc Em, an established musician who wrote his own music which came under the category of techno rock, and he used a sampler to make electronic sounds. They got signed by V2 records and made a couple of albums and although Tom stayed working at Eastenders he played at a lot of music festivals.

They had a gig in Lille one Saturday night and all the day staff from Eastenders wanted to go and see Tom playing, so they borrowed the company mini-bus and off we went to Lille. After the gig the staff went home and I waited for Tom and we packed his drum kit into the car, but we weren't going anywhere as the clutch cable broke and we had to spend the night in the car and get an early train to Calais in time for work at 8. When Dave West arrived, he asked Tom to go to his office and sacked him for taking his entire day staff away, and if something had happened he would be without staff. Tom was not particularly bothered and soon found a new job round the corner from Eastenders - another beer and wine warehouse owned by a man from Pakistan. Once Dave West got wind of where Tom was working he sacked me too. I worked there till the end of the day as I needed the 200 francs, but he made that last day miserable and wouldn't let me use the toilet. He told me to go and use the 'Pakis' toilet where Tom was working. In fact I did more than that, I got a job there too.

I was working in the cash desk and took the money for the sales and Tom was stacking the beer. We got paid £30 a day which was a great improvement on our finances. There was a Scottish man who worked there with a French wife who worked in the office. There was CCTV everywhere, and after a few days I noticed that the Scottish man was putting beer packs into the backs of vans which had not been paid for, so for verification I asked a couple of other staff members to come and look at the monitor. Sure enough we witnessed several cases of Strong Brew going into the back of a white van and all of a sudden the French wife burst into the kiosk and turned the monitor off telling us we had no right to look at it.

The following week we were told we were no longer needed. Tom wasn't bothered as he was soon to be on tour promoting Marc Em's new album 'Hybrid'.

So that was that. No job and we were soon going to be homeless and I would have no money to rent anywhere.

Chapter 25 - A House is Not Necessarily a Home

January 1999 we were in the depths of winter. I was desperate to find a job and with only 50 francs to my name I drove to Calais to a Beer and Wine warehouse owned by a nice man called Ravi and asked him if he could give me a job, but he said he couldn't as it was January and he had been laying his staff off. I got on my knees and begged him for a job, but he said it was impossible at this time of year but he would help me. He went to his office and came back with 1200 francs and put it in my hand, he said that he knew I wouldn't be able to pay him back but he made me promise that I would always be kind and helpful to people that were in difficult situations, a promise that I have kept all my life. Ravi's act of kindness made my life so much easier for a while and I was eternally grateful to him.

For 9 weeks Tom was the bread winner. He was playing in various European countries with Marc Em, promoting their album that had just been released, which included two television performances, he was coming home in between concerts.

It was up to me to find us somewhere to live and I had to rely on Tom to pay the deposit and the rent.

I found a 'cottage' to rent in Wideham, which is where we had spent New Year's Eve, at Pierrot's bar. It was a pretty little village and Etaples and Le Touquet were just a couple of miles down the road.

I went to visit the new home, which was owned by a strange man called Patrick. It was the worst place I had ever seen in my life, a half converted cowshed with one light bulb to light the entire building. It was all on one floor and there was a large tiled kitchen, which was where the one light bulb was, and a bathroom off it with an electric toilet, then off the kitchen a small entrance hall going into the lounge which had a large hole in the wall open to the elements. There was foliage and brambles growing down through the rafters and several snails slithering across the wall. Down a few steps was a bedroom with a door into the next bedroom and another door into the next bedroom. All three rooms had wall to wall concrete flooring and must have been the cubicles for the cows to sleep at night time.

As ghastly as it was I said we would take it as the rent was a mere 2,500 francs a month and because there was only one electricity metre it was agreed that we would give Patrick 300 francs a month towards the electricity. Patrick said he would fill in the hole in the wall and put some more lighting in and get rid of the snails and brambles that were growing inside. We agreed that we would move in on 1st. April.

Patrick was a strange man; he didn't have a job and spent his days creating a butterfly farm in the huge barn in the courtyard. I was given a tour of the barn, which was just dug up bits of earth and wires hanging like washing lines and some dead looking plants. He told me he was going to fill it with chrysalises which he was going to buy from abroad and soon there would be exotic butterflies filling the barn and he would open it to the public and there would be queues of people wanting to visit it.

The house in Wierre Effroy had been such a lovely house, the place where I was going to grow old in, but now it looked old and neglected. The conifers I had planted in the front garden all those years ago had never been pruned and were at least thirty feet high, the flower beds were long gone and the shutters had never had a drop of stain on them so the wood was dry and flaking. It looked such a sad house and was in need of a lot of loving care to restore it back to the days of when it was first built. I felt ashamed that I had let the house get into such a state but I had not the money nor inclination to maintain it.

We left the house in Wierre Effroy with a sense of relief as it had become a place of bad memories and huge debt and in turn we left a huge pile of rubbish in the front garden for the dustmen to pick up and dispose of.

I had managed to hang on to the wood burner so at least we would have some warmth.
The new house was dank and inhospitable but I was determined to make it as comfortable as I could. Patrick installed the wood burner which I lit straight away to air the damp building in which we were now living, and gradually I unpacked the stuff and it felt a bit more homely.

I desperately needed a job and I had to find one. Tom was paying for everything and at 19 years old should not have been keeping his mother. An American girl who had worked for a short while at Eastenders had told me about a beer warehouse owned by a couple of English brothers from Sunderland on the next industrial estate after Eastenders and I could try there for a job.

I found the place and it looked very messy with piles of plastic, empty beer cans and cigarette ends all over the floor and piled up in corners. It needed a good tidy up. I walked through the warehouse and called out to see if anyone was around but there was no answer. I went through a door into a corridor and then I could see the outline of someone in an office behind translucent glass, so I knocked and walked in and there, sitting behind a desk, was a man in his late 50's with a credit card in his hand chopping up white powder with his head just above the desk. He pushed one of his nostrils closed and snorted the white powder up the other. I nearly vomited it was a disgusting sight that I never would wish to witness. However, after he had finished snorting, he smiled and asked me what I wanted. I said I'd come to tidy up the warehouse, and he asked me if Stuart had sent me. I had no idea who Stuart was so I said yes, he had.

So I found a broom, a shovel and a roll of bin bags and began the mammoth task of clearing up months of mess. It took me all the afternoon, nearly four hours, but after I had finished it looked quite tidy, and Clive, the snorting man was pleased. He asked me how much money I would like and I said £35 would be enough and I asked him if he would like me to come back tomorrow, and he would!

The next day he sent me up some winding stairs to clean what was like living accommodation with a bit of a kitchen and five beds with dirty duvets screwed up on each one, cigarette ends and beer cans everywhere, and a sink full of dirty dishes with mouldy food stuck on them. I cleaned it all up, hoping to impress my new boss Clive. So I went back the next day and the next and Clive paid me £35 a day, then on the Saturday he told me he wouldn't be there the following week and that Stuart would be. He wasn't sure if Stuart would want me there full time or pay me the same as he had, but I should go in anyway.

I worried all the next day whether my job was going to come to an abrupt end. I got there early and there was a new man in the office who I presumed was Stuart and the work force had increased considerably. I introduced myself and he asked me if Clive had employed me to which I said yes and told him I had cleaned the whole building including the living quarters which no doubt belonged to the young men milling about everywhere. He asked me if I could drive a forklift truck, and I lied that I had a few years ago and would just need a quick reminder. I had seen the boys at Eastenders driving forklift trucks every day and it looked easy enough to me.

Some young man took me outside and piled up some empty pallets and showed me how to place the forks in the gaps and move one at a time to make a new pile, keeping them as straight as possible. I then lifted them up higher and placed them on top of another pile, so he left me to practise. It was easy and I had got the hang of it in no time. I could see in the warehouse that the beer was stacked four pallets high. The stronger beer like Special Brew was stacked on Euro pallets, 80 cases on each pallet and the lighter lagers like Carling were stacked onto chep pallets, 100 cases, the reason being that the stronger beers were heavier than the light lagers.

So the routine was Stuart was there one week with an abundance of staff and Clive was there the following week on his own. The job of Stuart's gang was to collect the orders and put the beer into the vans or cars, and there were only a couple of them allowed on the forklift trucks as the others were either too drunk or too stupid. I was relieved I had landed myself a job and I was probably the most intelligent one there, so I was soon unloading lorries in 20 minutes and stacking the beer four pallets high with amazing precision and loading empty pallets on to lorries, the chep pallets 15 high and the Euro pallets 20. I never dropped a pallet, but did puncture a few cases, which would send a cascade of beer flowing down onto the warehouse floor. I cleaned and kept the place tidy.

I gradually became acquainted with my bizarre new colleagues with strange accents which were difficult to understand. The word that was spoken the most was 'fucker' but they didn't even manage to pronounce that correctly it was more like 'fooka', and 'why aye man you fooka" was the most spoken phrase. They walked everywhere with their hands down the fronts of their track suit bottoms fiddling with whatever was down there and had an extraordinary method of blowing their noses which was quite revolting, pressing one nostril closed with their finger and blowing the slimy contents out of the other nostril onto the floor and wiping away any residue with the back of the hand. It was of no consequence whether this act was performed outside or inside. Some told me they used to work on the ferries, so I thought my opinion of them had perhaps been a bit harsh and there was some intelligence in there somewhere, but that feeling was soon dispelled as the 'work' transpired to be carrying large quantities of cigarette cartons back to the UK and smuggling them through the customs for Stuart.

Stuart used to sell cigarettes to his customers and the odd wrap of cocaine, but that was not my business and I didn't care what he was doing.

Before long Tom came to work there too and was put on the night shift. Stuart soon realised that compared to the majority of his staff Tom could add up, speak French and English, drive a forklift truck and was versatile in all aspects of running a ware-house. So Tom with his feet comfortably under the table meant Stuart could go to bed at night time and leave Tom in the office dealing with the orders and taking the money and a couple of employees loading the vans and cars.

So for the time being we had secure jobs, one week with Stuart and one week with Clive. I could hear Clive and Stuart arguing a lot on change over day and eventually Clive stopped coming and it was down to Stuart and his mentally challenged younger brother Stephen to run the place on alternate weeks.

I had a day off and Tom was on day shift when suddenly, in the middle of the afternoon, Clive, accompanied by one male and one female French legal representative and two thugs brandishing baseball bats burst into the office. Tom was commandeered to act as translator while the two French men served some papers on Stuart demanding that he signed the business over to Clive who was now the new owner. As soon as Stuart had signed the document the two French people took it and hurried away to safety and as soon as they had left the two thugs replaced their baseball bats with handguns and ordered everyone to leave the building except Tom. Stuart left, taking his baffled work force with him, and they drove off while Tom was left alone with Clive and the two thugs.

Customers came and went, and Tom served them and took the money which he was ordered to hand over to Clive. In the meantime Stuart had rung Clive and they were negotiating over the phone. When there were plenty of customers Tom managed to stuff some of the money down his trousers. At around 9 o'clock one of Stuart's sidekicks came into the warehouse and bought a case of beer but it was really to check that Tom was OK. The siege came to an end in the early hours of the morning when Clive and Stuart had come to an agreement and Clive left taking his thugs and a large bundle of cash with him. Shortly after Stuart and his entourage arrived back at the warehouse and Tom was pleased to be able to give Stuart about £2000 he had managed to salvage. Stuart didn't give Tom a penny for his courage.

Not long after that, as things were chugging along nicely, Tom and a couple of workers were there one night, when Stuart rang him to say that a guy called Tony Ballony was coming with £39,000 pounds for cigarettes and asked Tom to count the money and put it back in the bag. The guy turned up and Tom counted the money all correct £39,000 and put it back in the bag and handed the bag back to the guy who he thought was off to pick up his cigarettes. When Stuart arrived back later that night he asked Tom where the money was and Tom innocently told him he had handed it back to the guy thinking he was going to buy his cigarettes with it, but the guy had already collected his cigarettes and Tom had inadvertently handed his money back to him. Not a great situation but there it was and it was too late to do anything about it, however rumour had it that the guy was stopped in Dover and had his haul and money taken off him.

Chapter 26 - Up Up and Away

Tom was getting bored with his job and the environment he was working in. Marc Em had decided to give up on their band and go and write jingles for video games, so Tom made the decision to try and get a place at Drum Tech in Acton, London. He needed two GCSE's to get into the school which he didn't have, but the head of Drum Tech said they would audition him instead. He was accepted on his drumming skills and he was booked in to start his drum course the following April 2000.

In the meantime our lives carried on in the warehouse in Calais until one day that was all going to change. I had seen a guy named Pav coming to the warehouse to see Clive on odd occasions, a huge man, very self-composed and well-spoken with a gentle voice, he used to come there to do the accounts for the business.

On this autumnal day with a chill in the air I was reminded that winter would soon be here and I would be unloading lorries and working in a freezing cold warehouse again. Then Pav came in and asked me if he could have a word. He offered me a driving job to Luxembourg three times a week to pick up cigarettes and tobacco and bring it back to Calais and he would pay me £300 a day. That was a no-brainer and I accepted the job in a split second. I couldn't wait to start. He said he would supply a rented car which he would change monthly and I could take it home and use at my pleasure.

I realised the risks that went with the job but I wasn't deterred by it at all. I had been living in penury for the last five years and now it was all going to change. The first trip I would go with a man they called 'The Cockney Wanker', who would show me the way and introduce me to the owners of the cigarette warehouse in Luxembourg.

I told Stuart I was off on a smuggling career and he was fine about it and Tom was forced into early retirement as I couldn't fit my hours in with his. At last I was on the brink of leaving poverty behind and about to embrace the 'life of Riley'.

It was October 1999 and I drove to Luxembourg accompanied by my mentor, 'The Cockney Wanker'. We left Calais early and I had to memorise the way as we drove straight onto the duel carriage way to Dunkirk into Belgium. Once in Belgium we detoured to a small town called Veurne where the British bought their cigarettes and tobacco, and pulled into a garage where there was a lady with whom we exchanged British pounds for Belgium francs. Back on the E411 the scenery was breath-taking, the many forests we passed en route were a blaze of autumnal colour and conversation with The Cockney Wanker was kept to a minimum as I was concentrating and remembering the route because he was only going to accompany me once, and besides he didn't have a lot to say that I understood anyway. We carried along the E411 until we reached the Brussels ring road, an amazing infrastructure six lanes wide with junctions every 500 metres for 75 kilometres. I approached it with great caution. The Cockney Wanker gave me directions and I managed to get to the other side with my nerves intact. We stopped at a Q8 Gas Station in Gembloux for a coffee and croissant, filled up with petrol for the return journey and continued to the Luxembourg border. I noticed there were plenty of police, douaniers and gendarmes loitering there. Once we got into Luxembourg we left the dual carriageway at Junction 3 in the direction of the cigarette warehouse. It had taken four hours to drive 425 kilometres. The Cockney Wanker had put the back seats down in his estate car, and we bought 10 boxes of cigarettes and 5 bags of tobacco and loaded the car, after which he put a black sheet over the top to cover it.

As we left on the return journey I felt apprehensive as we approached the Luxembourg/ Belgium border. The Cockney Wanker told me not drive too fast, not to look guilty and not to make eye contact with the douaniers or gendarmes who were waiting to pounce on the British smugglers. My throat was dry, my hands were sweaty and my heart was thumping as we drove over the border. I tried so very hard not to look guilty but the feeling of sheer terror must have been plastered all over my face. With great relief we crossed the border without any problems and arrived back in Calais five hours later. The next time I drove to Luxembourg I would be alone.

And the next time was a couple of days later. Pav had given me £6000 to change into Belgian francs and a very nice silver Renault Scenic with the back seats removed and a large black sheet. I left at 7 a.m. and did the same routine as I had with The Cockney Wanker, changed the money, managed the Brussels ring road and stopped for coffee and filled up with petrol. The load was more this time and I packed it all into the back of the car, covered it with the black sheet and remembering what The Cockney Wanker had told me I nervously crossed the border into Belgium again with a dry mouth, sweaty hands and a thumping heart.

I was the happiest person alive, my best paid job ever, so easy, no one breathing down my neck and I could start what time I chose, but I preferred to leave early. Another bonus was that the pound was really low and when I changed the pounds into francs I made another £60 or £70 on top.

I did the trip three times a week to start off with, earning over £1000 a week, which would previously have taken me 5 weeks to earn. Every week I bought an electrical appliance, video camera, clothes, food, fine dining, shoes, furniture, till there was nothing else to buy. But I still had that dry mouth, thumping heart and those sweaty hands crossing the border into Belgium.

With all the money I was earning we had made the once inhospitable cowshed into a warm and cosy home and Christmas 1999 was the best we had had in years, a Christmas tree, a huge Christmas dinner and presents for everyone and a roaring log fire throughout. It was a happy time for us at last. For the new year we went to Hastings to celebrate the new millennium with friends, and as we sang Auld Lang Syne I had a sudden longing to come back to live in England.

But once back in France I got ready to return to work and earn lots of money, and the idea of moving back to England had for the moment subsided.

Then on the 28th February 2000 the UK announced that the strict quarantine laws that had been in place for decades where an animal on returning to the UK from abroad would have to be put into kennels for 6 months had now been replaced with a less expensive alternative whereby the animal would have to be micro-chipped, tattooed and vaccinated against rabies, blood tested six months after the vaccination and have a vet do a health check 24 hours before departure to the UK. Nicor had all the requirements apart from the blood test so that meant I could now if I wanted to return to England with him rather than having to wait for him to die.

One morning in February I left home at 4 a.m. to go to Luxembourg, as I needed to be back home early that afternoon. I arrived in good time and as I got into the house I realised there was no electricity. I went and knocked on Patrick's door and asked him what was happening and he told me there was a problem with the supply. I decided I would go to visit the EDF in Le Touquet to find out what was going on. I was told that the bill had not been paid and the supply had been disconnected. I was furious and explained that I was a tenant and that I paid 300 francs a month for our share of electricity. Eventually it was agreed that I would make the payment directly to the EDF instead of Patrick and they would reconnect the supply.

It had become quite obvious that our landlord Patrick was somewhat mentally deficient, what with his huge barn full of dead and dying butterflies and his childlike drawings of a strange looking oblong he had put up all over the village saying 'Suivre la Chenille' in English 'Follow the caterpillar'. I chose not to tell him of this new arrangement in case it caused him to have a tantrum, which he had demonstrated on several occasions when he couldn't get his own way.

He must have been very surprised when the electricity came back on but didn't mention anything to us until he wanted his 300 francs. It was raining hard one night and Patrick came banging on the front door demanding his 300 francs and when I told him of the new arrangement with EDF he became agitated and was there in the garden in the rain having a tantrum. He just happened to be standing by my rotary washing line so as he was ranting and raving at me I grabbed hold of the end of it and gave it a mighty shove which set it spinning and whacked Patrick on the side of his head, clearly hurting him as he put his hand up to nurse his throbbing ear. He then became more outraged. Tom, hearing all the commotion, came charging out of the house with a cricket bat and held it under Patrick's chin threatening to hit him with it if he didn't go away and stop harassing us. He went rubbing his painful ear.

A few days later Annie the little Staff had gone walk-abouts into the village and Tom and I spent most of the day walking round Wideham calling her but there was no sign. I was getting anxious and feared she might have jumped into the back of a van or truck and by evening there was still no sign of her, as I put the food into Nicor's bowl I heard Annie whining and it was coming from Patrick's house next door. Tom went straight round there and banged on his door, which he eventually opened and Annie came tearing out into the open having been cooped up in there with Patrick all day poor dog. Patrick claimed to have found her walking around the village and hadn't realised we were in, which was utter rubbish. Of course it was retaliation for his 300 francs going towards what it was meant for.

Pav had hired a splendid Volvo C80 with blue with white leather upholstery but the problem was it was automatic and I had never driven an automatic car before, so we met at 6 o'clock one icy morning in the car park of the 'Le Clerc' supermarket in Boulogne and he gave me a crash course on how to drive it. I had to keep my left foot busy to start off with to stop it from using the break as a clutch.

Wow this was the life! I was driving posh cars and earning more money than I could spend quickly enough. The years of penury were just a distant memory and I felt like a millionaire. I was braving the border, but the fear did not get any better and the sweaty hands, dry throat and pumping heart didn't go away. I bought large bags of chocolate M&M's, and crammed as many as I could into my mouth to cross the border which hopefully changed the look on my face from fear to that of a hamster.

Then one day, as I was on my return journey driving along the E411 about 100 kilometres from the Brussels ring road I was nabbed, pulled over by the Belgium douanes. I was going to say that the 40,000 cigarettes and 25 bags of Golden Virginia on board were for my own personal use but I didn't think they would believe me, so I tried a different tactic by pleading ignorance to the fact that I was breaking any laws. So I was carted all the way back to Arlon, chauffeured by a douanier, as he wouldn't let me drive, and we followed behind the other one. When we arrived a group of douaniers set about emptying the car of its contraband while I was put in a room and questioned. I said it wasn't my stuff and that I worked for someone but I didn't know his name. I asked them if I was going to be in trouble but to my surprise they said being caught smuggling was like having a back light not working. They would tell me once but then if they caught me again the consequences would be more severe than the last time and that I had seven chances before I went to prison, plus if the duty was paid on this load I could have it back. I only had to return there with the money. I got back really late that day as I was detained in Arlon for a good three hours. Pav had guessed that something had happened, but gave me the money to go back the following day to retrieve the confiscated goods.

The next day Pav changed the hire car to a Renault Espace but he had trouble hiring it as the French car hire companies had cottoned on to the antics of the English cigarette smugglers which not only put the cars at risk of being impounded but they were clocking up thousands upon thousands of kilometres on their vehicles prematurely depreciating the value of the cars.

Jean-Paul, my partner in crime who smuggled the cigarettes and tobacco into England, came up with a genius idea to defraud the car hire companies. He took a long piece of flexible wire and connected a push button switch one end and a car fuse the other, as the Renault Espace clocked up the kilometres in digital. Removing the indicator fuse and inserting the wire in its place with the switch off would stop the kilometres mounting up but at the same time it would stop the indicator lights working too, so the switch would have to be clicked on every time it was needed to indicate. I soon got into a rhythm and turning the switch on and off to indicate became the norm.

After getting busted I found another way back onto the E411 which meant I took the scenic route as soon as I had gone over the border into Belgium. I found a turn-off which went off into the countryside and was never manned by police. It ran parallel with the E411, passing through several small villages, and 80 kilometres later it eventually came back onto the E411, so for a while I took this root.

One day I went to pick up a small load compared to what I usually brought back. I was driving an estate car. Once loaded up I took my usual safe scenic route through the villages but just on the road to get back onto the E411 there was a lay-by with three gendarmes with motorbikes searching vehicles. I was directed to pull in and wait my turn for whatever was going to happen. To my horror the driver of the car in front of me was made to get out of his car and open the boot, and I thought 'if I am made to do that I would fake a heart attack', which I felt I might have been heading for anyway as my heart was thumping so much you could see my coat going in and out. I did not turn off the engine nor did I remove my foot from the clutch, I remained in first gear and my leg was shaking like a jelly.

Then the gendarme came to me and indicated for me to open the window, with my foot shaking on the clutch I looked at the gendarme afraid to speak. He asked to see my driving licence and the papers for the car. I fumbled about in my bag and gave him my English driving licence, still covered in the graffiti I had written on it to annoy the Gestapo. The gendarme was keen to practise his English and said 'Ah English'. 'Yes' I said, 'car papers please' he said and I rummaged in the glove compartment for the hire papers which were in Pav's name and handed them to him. He took the papers and walked round the car peering in the side windows and saw nothing because everything was in the boot, he walked round again this time checking the vignette (tax disc) on the windscreen, then again he walked round the car, and by this time my leg and foot on the clutch were in agony and had not stopped shaking the whole while. Finally, he came back to the window and handed everything back to me and said 'enjoy your holiday madam'. I couldn't wait to get away quick enough and into fifth gear so I could take my foot off the clutch and relax my leg. Realising how lucky I had been I drove as quickly as I dared, with my heart thumping, all the way back to Calais.

Chapter 27 - Nothing Lasts Forever

The time came for Tom to return to England and I was very sad to see him go, but at the same time I was proud of his achievement in his drumming career. So there I was alone in France with Nicor, my German Shepherd, who would sometimes accompany me on my smuggling trips. He was a heavy dog so when the Espace was first packed it was stacked right up to the ceiling so with the black cover over it Nicor would lie on top and flatten the load. I hoped he would act as a deterrent and the douanes would think twice before stopping me with a large dog in the car.

On one trip Pav had hired a brand new Alfa Romeo with leather seats and six forward gears - another beautiful car. I had packed all the cigarettes and tobacco into the boot and some on the back seat covered in the black sheet. I took the scenic route as usual, and when I got to one of the villages I couldn't believe my eyes - the whole village had been dug up, probably for re-surfacing the old worn out roads. There was no way I was going to turn round and go back so I drove slowly to see if I could find a way out, and there all of a sudden was a dirt track and I felt sure it would come out the other side of the village. I bumped down the track and eventually was heading towards a pine forest, but I kept going and as I entered the forest it became quite dark and so I had to put the headlights on. As I drove on into the thick of the forest I noticed the track was becoming narrower and before long was just a foot path. I couldn't turn round now even if I wanted to and the thought of me driving this brand new Alfa Romeo through a forest with the head lights on was making me laugh, as the game plan was to not draw attention to myself and here I was in this awkward predicament trying to be discreet. I carried on and it seemed I had been driving along this footpath in the shadows of the pine trees forever and then, much to my relief, through the tree trunks I saw a glimmer of sun light, and as the footpath began to get slowly wider I eventually bumped my way off the dirt track onto a proper road which felt so good to drive on, then back onto the E411 and home.

After that it was back to the Espace with the seats taken out and transporting my 40,000 cigarettes and 25 bags of rolling tobacco. I had been driving in all sorts of conditions. There was something about the Belgium roads that made driving in rain a hazard as the rain water settled on the road surface and with lorries passing the other side of the motorway they would send waves of water covering the entire car and even with the windscreen wipers on full pelt it was impossible to see where you were going for a brief moment. Overtaking lorries was another hazard with the car being engulfed in rainwater, but I got used to the dangers and just used to grit my teeth and go for it.

One very hot day I had left Nicor at home as it would have been too uncomfortable for him to be stuck in the car in such heat for 9 hours. So this day I travelled alone. I had collected my load and as usual just before the border I went to stuff a handful of m&m's into my mouth, but realised I had not opened the bag. I tried to open it with one hand but it was impossible, so trying to steer I grabbed the m&m's bag and yanked at it, it burst open and 500 m&m's went flying everywhere. I started to panic, sweaty hands, dry mouth my heart was thumping. I needed to fill my mouth with some m&m's which were all over the floor and dash board, I quickly scooped a handful up from the passenger seat and stuffed them into my mouth just as I reached the border crossing.

I was not going to stop to pick up all the m&m's that were rolling around on the floor and dash board, as they would just have to melt in the hot sun but I did try to eat as many as I could reach.

By the time I got back onto the E411 I had recovered from the m&m trauma and was heading for the Brussels ring road. I had only a short distance to go when all of a sudden a douane van appeared from nowhere and blocked me, causing me to pull up onto the hard shoulder.

My first reaction was to disconnect the wire which was coming out of the fuse box as that would have been a fraudulent offence which I could have been in trouble for. I had no time to replace the missing fuse. The two douaniers had got out of their van and were heading towards me and I was desperately trying to push the never-ending wire under my seat. I didn't know why it had to be so long. I opened the window and smiled sweetly at the two douaniers. One told me to get out and open the side door, but I couldn't as the boxes of cigarettes were piled up against it so I opened the back revealing the 40,000 cigarettes and 25 bags of Golden Virginia hidden under the black sheet. I didn't say a word and I looked at the douanier and then I looked in the back of the Espace and then back at the douanier. He asked me if the tobacco was for my own use 'of course it is' I said, then they muttered something to each other and one said to me, 'we don't believe you, you will have to accompany us back to Arlon'. God I was fed up! That was 200 kilometres and a 2-hour drive back from where I had just come.

In the normal scheme of things, when one was nabbed in this situation one douanier would drive in front and the other would drive your vehicle, but as luck would have it my douanier had been shot in the eye and only had one, making him unfit to drive or have a gun, so I had to drive my own car with him in the passenger seat. I was so relieved as I still had a good couple of metres of wire to stuff under my seat. I apologised for the m&m's which were all over the floor and told him he could help himself if he wanted to. The ones on the dashboard were in various stages of melt down, all the blue ones had melted first, and the brown and green ones had changed their shape to flat, but the red and yellow ones were still intact.

As I was going to spend a good two hours with this man, I got chatting to him and at the same time I discreetly tried to stuff the remaining wire under my seat. He told me how he had lost his eye and had nearly died from the wound. His name was Julien, he had been a douane most of his life and he was 52 years old and married. By the time we got back to Arlon we were the best of mates, but I still had the worry of keeping the wire hidden, so as soon as we stopped I said I would empty the car for them. I had pushed the wire for so long it was now poking out the back of the seat so I stuffed it back under as I unloaded the cigarettes and bags of tobacco. It was all carried into the office where I was in for the usual questioning. I answered the same as I had before, I didn't know who I worked for or where the tobacco was going to end up. They knew this was the second time they had caught me and said my lives were running out. Nevertheless if the duty was paid then I could have it all back like the last time. So once again I went back to Calais with an empty car, but Pav was not really bothered. I guess he was making so much money that a couple of thousand pounds was not a lot to lose.

After that I decided I was not going to take the E411 route back to Calais and I found another way out of Luxembourg that went directly into France but it meant driving 250 kilometres through French villages and then 320 kilometres on the autoroute from Reims to Calais. The only drawback with that was I had to stop and pay at the end of the Péage in St. Omer where there were lots of police, douaniers and gendarmes waiting to pounce on the British smugglers. Pav got me a Sanef card which was a card that you swiped through a machine when you arrived at the end of the Péage and was located away from the other tolls and no one ever stood guard there and once a month Pav would receive a bill for the amount of times I had used it. My only anxiety was that I feared that when I arrived there in St. Omer, I might drop the Sanef card.

So I continued to take the scenic route through France and it worked. Sometimes there were gendarmes at the Luxembourg French border but with my mouth stuffed with m&m's I passed them by without any trouble. Once I got to Lille on the Péage it was 25 minutes to St. Omer and I still got the dry mouth and sweaty hand syndrome plus the thumping heart. One day with Nicor in the back flattening the load we were en route between Lille and St. Omer, Nicor woke up and decided he was going to do a circular stretch and in doing so he took the black sheet with him exposing all the tobacco and boxes of cigarettes. I panicked, I didn't know whether I should carry on regardless or stop in a lay-by and cover it over again. Quite often the douaniers waited in the lay-bys just before St. Omer ready to chase anyone they considered suspicious. There was no way off the autoroute and so they would be trapped by the time they got to the end of the Péage. I carried on driving for a while knowing I had to make a decision because although I had slowed down to give myself time to think the end of the Péage was fast approaching. I decided to pull in to a lay-by. I left the engine running and jumped into the back of the Espace and tried to cover the load, but with a 50 kilo dog sitting on it, it wasn't easy. In my fluster I dropped my phone down between the boxes, but covered everything up the best I could. I went through the toll safely and then drove like a bat out of hell all the way back to Calais.

I had made so much money I had stuffed it into carrier bags and put it under my bed. I couldn't put it in a bank as I had lost my bank account when I had been made bankrupt. I was living a luxurious life which had made up for the 5 years of poverty, losing the shop, losing the house, working in that awful Eastenders with all those weirdos, then the warehouse with those ignorant people from Sunderland and the scum of the earth who had held Tom hostage.

My life was fabulous until November 7th, 2000 when my best paid job came to an abrupt end. Jean-Paul was nabbed in Folkstone and arrested for smuggling. They had been eyeballing him for months and he was sentenced to 18 months in Canterbury jail. In a way I was glad it was him and not me, but my life of luxury was going to slowly return to what it had been before once all my bagged-up money had run out.

Chapter 28 - He who Dares

In the new year I decided that I would go and ask Stuart if I could drive to Luxembourg for him and collect the tobacco and cigarettes but he said he had enough runners for that, but he did have an alternative proposition to make. He said he would rent a house for me to live in and as his runners returned from Luxembourg they would drop the tobacco off for me to look after until it was needed at the warehouse where I would deliver it. He would pay me £200 a week as well which I felt was not very much compared to the £1000 or more I had been used to earning, and it would also mean moving, but I didn't mind that really as Tom was not here anymore and Wideham was quite a long way from Calais.

That decided, we found a house not far from Dunkirk in a tiny village called Oye Plage where nothing ever happened, which made the landlord highly suspicious as to why a single English woman would want to rent a large house in such a quiet place where the sand dunes in the garden backed onto the beach. But that's the way it was and I left our cowshed in Wideham and the nutty landlord Patrick into a much grander house with a huge garden walled by tall poplar trees, where the leaves were constantly rustling from the breeze which blew off La Manche (the English Channel).

I was wanting to return to England now more than ever. I missed my children so much, and I could not see any future here doing this job, which sooner or later was going to come to an abrupt end like my smuggling job, so I decided to have Nicor blood tested for rabies just in case, and besides that would be at least six months before I could go anywhere with him.

I was still having quite a cushy life despite the mighty drop in wages, but I was kept busy with the nightly deliveries of tobacco and cigarettes which I hid in the back of a van which was tucked away in the garage in the garden. Unfortunately the house next door which also had a large garden was frequently occupied by the owners eating every meal of the day at a garden table just beside the fence in full view of my garage which was annoying, for when I was asked to deliver to the warehouse I wasn't always able to complete the mission, as the neighbours could see everything I was doing. So it was a matter of waiting for them to finish their meal and retire into their house.

Although my life was secure for the time being, it was dull and I missed the excitement of ducking and diving from the authorities, but then one day I was en route with a delivery for the warehouse in Calais when I noticed that there had been a man in a red Peugeot 106 driving behind me for some time and I became suspicious and rang Stuart and told him. He told me to go back to Oye Plage and he would catch me up, so I detoured back onto the carriageway with the Peugeot still following. As I turned off into the lane I was still being followed. I could not go home as he would realise where the stash was so instead of turning into the drive of the house I carried on and drove back towards the duel carriageway. All the while the red Peugeot was behind. As I drove back onto the main road I saw Stuart in my wing mirror who had now caught up and was behind the Peugeot. He told me I must drive towards Belgium because once I was there it was not in the jurisdiction of the French authorities, and sure enough as I drove over the border into Belgium the red Peugeot drove off at the next junction and back towards France.

One day I was beckoned to the warehouse and was introduced to one of Stuart's friends, Ali from Manchester, the plan being that Stuart was going to create another warehouse in Calais and it was going to be in Ali's name. As I spoke French he wanted me to go and register the new business and to do all the ground work. He also wanted us to go to various businesses and open credit accounts with them. Ali told me that Stuart had promised to pay him £100,000 for his trouble, but it sounded a bit dodgy to me.

Stuart had found a warehouse in Calais for rental and it was huge. First of all we went to the Chambre de Commerce in Calais to register the business, then with proof of the business on paper we went to Cite Europe in Coquelles and with the list of businesses Stuart had given us we proceeded to trek from one shop to another asking for credit, but we didn't have much luck apart from one shop called Tandy that sold computers, laptops, printers and all manner of electrical office equipment, who agreed to give credit up to 50,000 francs. Stuart compiled lists of beer and wine for Ali to contact various suppliers with the orders with the intention of building up a good credit account with them.

Then Stuart wanted me to drive to Lille to the Ikea there and open up a credit account. He told me he wanted the nice Ikea furniture to fit out the office in the new building and as a reward he said I could have a new sofa. My mission to Ikea was successful and I got Stuart another 50,000 francs credit.

As time went by the new warehouse was up and running and Stuart asked me to go to Lille to get him chairs for the new office and told me to grab myself a sofa. I would never say I was a greedy person but the thought of going to Ikea with a huge amount of credit at my disposal was unfortunately leading me into temptation, so I went and hired a long backed transit van and set off full of excitement to Lille.

Once in there I parked up in the huge Ikea car park and grabbed a trolley and went on the biggest spending spree of my life. First I got Stuart's chairs which were in flat packs and stacked nicely on the trolley floor, then I went and chose two identical sofas in cream and a mattress for my bed which would be collected at the end of my shop. After that I just followed the yellow brick road, grabbing as much as I could balance on the huge pile of purchases I had made. Rugs, coffee table, cushions, bed linen, pillows, pots and pans, pictures, kitchen utensils, chopping boards, ornaments, until I could get no more to balance on the trolley.

Queuing at the checkout I got the vapours a bit feeling slightly guilty, but I calmed down by convincing myself that Stuart would be paying the bill for all this stuff though I had a feeling he might not. I paid with the Ikea credit card and went to collect the sofas and mattress which were brought out on a fork lift truck and dumped on the ground, I loaded the back of the van on my own in a disorganised fashion but I was strong through working in the warehouse and managed to stuff everything in. My next mission was to get it all back to Oye Plage and into the house without anyone seeing my purchases, especially Stuart or those divs that drove to Luxembourg for him. So I emptied everything into the house except Stuart's chairs and one sofa. I drove to the warehouse and delivered the two chairs making sure the one sofa was seen in the back of the van. Mission accomplished.

A few days later Stuart's brother and a couple of others asked if they could borrow my car to listen to a Sunderland match on the radio. I agreed and left my car at the warehouse for them. The next day I found my car trashed, they had pulled the radio out of its socket, removed the head rests from the seats and chucked them away somewhere, left empty beer cans and cigarette ends and burns everywhere. I was furious and this wasn't the first time they had wrecked my car, as when I had the white Astra they had picked it up on two fork lift trucks and dropped it and then rammed it all over making dents in it. I went and told Stuart and he didn't care what his brother had done.

I saw Ali from time to time. I would pop into his warehouse for a chat and he was telling me how pleased he was by getting a huge amount of credit deals with the beer suppliers which was what Stuart had told him to do, but he was worried, as Stuart had not yet given him the £100,000 he had promised him. One time I went there and the warehouse was stocked up to the ceiling. I didn't stop long as Stuart's brother had a gun and was shooting at the pallets of beer, exploding the beer cans so the beer was flowing across the floor and I didn't want to get roped in to clearing it up.

A few days later when I was delivering some bags of tobacco Stuart handed me a large pile of documents and folders and told me to dispose of it all, I asked him where he wanted me to put it and he told me to bury it in the garden as burning it might attract attention and there was tons of it. At home I went into the garden and started to dig a hole but it was tiring and so I looked at some of the documents Stuart had given me and there were loads of export documents and invoices for the transportation of beer. I couldn't be bothered to dig the hole so I just took the pile indoors and left it there. The next time I went to see Ali his warehouse was empty and no sign of Ali so I guessed the documents Stuart had given me were connected to this business and that he had sold the stock and done a runner. Poor Ali, everything was in his name.

Chapter 29 - Hell Hath No Fury

I had worked really hard for Stuart over the months and I was angry with him for not caring about his brother and chums wrecking my cars. I thought after my loyalty and honesty he might have been a bit more concerned. One time I had found a wad of two thousand pounds lying on the floor in the office and given it straight back to him, and after Tom had managed to save some of his money as well as being held hostage he had given him no reward what so ever, so it was time to get my own back and I was out for revenge. I had the most brilliant idea on how to do it but I would need an accomplice and what better person to ask than Pav.

It was April and I ran my idea past Pav. He was up for aiding and abetting me in my plan but we decided to bide our time until we would be in a position to make the biggest gain.

I carried on the normal routine ducking and a diving from the douanes, looking forward to retribution day. Then in July as a change of routine Stuart commissioned me to deliver £37,000 cash to a man in a lay-by opposite a petrol station in Strood. I willingly obliged and took the money in a large brown envelope. I had no idea what it was for but the mission was successful and I returned to France.

As we got to August Pav and I decided it was soon going to be payback time and in advance Pav hired a white transit van and we waited. Then on August 19th. 2001 we put our plan into action.

I waited for the last driver to drop off his load of tobacco. He got there at about 10.30pm. I wanted him to know that I was going to visit a friend so I moaned at him for being late as I was driving to Condette to see my friend Susan. After he had gone I called Pav to tell him the last drop off had been delivered. He was not far away and after a few minutes, with headlights off he drove slowly into the driveway and parked by the garage, where there lay £22,000 worth of cigarettes and tobacco for the taking. I joined Pav and opened the garage doors and then the back door of the van, and we quickly set about unloading the tobacco and loading it into Pav's hire van. When we had finished I locked the van up and then locked the garage doors. Pav went to the front of his van and produced a roughneck crowbar and forced the garage door open. and then did the same to the small van inside, making sure he caused as much damage as he could. Job done he pushed the garage doors together and Pav drove off to Wimereaux with the haul and I drove to Condette to see Susan regardless of the time.

I knew the next day I would have to do my best Oscar winning role to convince Stuart and his brother and father that the robbery was nothing to do with me. The next day when the inevitable phone call came asking me to take five bags of tobacco down to the warehouse I went into acting mode, 'Won't be long' I told Stuart as I made my way to the garage.

From the moment I went into the garden and despite having no audience I did my best acting role. I was shocked to see the state of the garage door and cautiously opened it and was horrified to see the back door of the van all bent and scratched, and, what's more, empty. God what had happened, who had done this? I ran into the house and rang Stuart and with a trembling incoherent voice I tried to tell him that there was no tobacco in the van, it was empty. He sounded very cross and told me I was fucking joking, I had to say I wasn't joking and in a tearful voice I told him to come and see for himself.

Within 20 minutes they arrived. Stuart and his brother went and checked the garage and the father Benny came charging into the house and I stood there shaking and snivelling until the other two joined him. Stuart straight away accused me of having something to do with the burglary and I defended myself by reminding him that he had given me £37,000 to take to a stranger in Strood a little while ago, so why on earth would I rob him of tobacco that I would have to get rid of. I told him the only person who knew I wouldn't be there last night was the last driver back, Mick, because I had told him I was going out, 'so it must have been him' I said accusingly. They wouldn't go and continued to accuse me of robbing them and then Stuart said I wouldn't want anything to happen to my children. I had no fear of that threat as he had no idea where either of them was but I acted scared and told him to leave my children out of this situation. Eventually they left, and Stuart said he would no longer be paying the rent on the house and if I wanted to stay there I would have to pay it myself.

I was so relieved when they had gone and was very proud of my Oscar winning performance. But with no time to spare I had to pack up and leave this house and make plans for my return to England.

Chapter 30 - There's No Place Like Home

The arrangement I had with Pav regarding our ill-gotten gains was that he would give me my share of the haul as he sold it, but to get myself and belongings back to the UK he gave me £1000 in advance. I had to wait one more month for Nicor to be given the all-clear for his passport, and hire a lorry to transport my goods and chattels to Hastings, plus someone who had an HGV licence to get it there.

In the meantime I was going to stay with my friend Susan in Condette. The removal was arranged quickly and I was relieved to get my Ikea purchases out of France. Within a week of the great tobacco robbery my goods and chattels were on their way back to the UK and I was safely hiding in Condette like a fugitive.

Nicor's blood test came back negative and I booked my ferry home. I had very little money left of the £1000 Pav had given me, by the time I had paid the hire of the lorry, the two guys and the return ferry fare, my ferry fare, plus the dog who cost 4 times more than me and the car put together.

The time went slowly while I stayed with Susan. She had no television and we used to take her dog for walks in the grounds of Chateau Hardelot where she'd make me hug trees, which was not my thing, but I obliged as I needed somewhere to stay.

The day before my departure the starter motor broke on the car so I had to phone around Boulogne to find someone to come and change it. A friend of Tom's turned up with one he had found in a breakers yard and thankfully changed it, so after I had paid him I only had 1000 francs left to my name.

Saturday 15th. September 2001 I was up very early. I had an appointment with a vet in Calais at 8 o'clock for Nicor's final check. I bade Susan farewell and thanked her for letting me stay, and I was on my way home at last. The vet checked Nicor for fleas and other maladies and issued him with a clean bill of health certificate and the yellow paper which was his passport. I had to pay 800 francs to the vet which included the check-up and passport papers.

I drove to Calais port and went through passport control showing my own and Nicor's passports. I was told to put my hazard lights on and got priority to board the ferry. I was ushered onto the ferry long before the other vehicles drove on. I was parked on the outside part of the deck so Nicor would have plenty of fresh air in the car. I was allowed to check on him twice accompanied by a crew member.

We set sail at 9.30am. I had mixed emotions as I reflected on my time in France. I had moved to France a respectable married woman and because of my reckless, selfish husband we had suffered much hardship. It was beyond my imagination why someone would abandon his family, who did not deserve such treatment, in a foreign country. By consequence I had become a rebel and a smuggler. I had done things I would never had dreamed of doing and gone from penury to wealth and back again, but I rode the tide and came out on the other side. I had happy and sad memories, had made some fabulous friends, met all manner of people, smoked pot, gone bankrupt, become a fast driver, learnt new cooking skills and learnt to speak a foreign language. I had changed forever. I had become tough, thankful for small mercies, thankful to Leonard Cohen for that song, and I had realised that there are more good people in the world than bad ones.

And now here I was on my way home in a car with no tax, insurance or MOT, a crack right across the middle of the windscreen, the petrol tank hanging down as one of the straps had broken, both the electric windows stuck at an angle half open, and £19 in my purse which would soon be £9 as I needed to buy petrol, and when I did get to the UK I had nowhere to go.

I went down to the deck to check on Nicor and I saw the white cliffs of Dover fast approaching. That dream of a new life in France when I had been so full of excitement and hope was over, and here I was just about to dock in Dover with memories such as I would never have imagined, but for me my life in France had come to an end.

THE END

Written by Sally Pattinson 20th. August 2019

Edited by Elizabeth Hojlund

Cover by Tom.